MW01098058

1650 Market Street Center City West
Suite 3600
Philadelphia, PA 19103

For information regarding special discounts for bulk purchases, contact LEADx® at:

Email: info@leadx.org

Web: www.LEADx.org

Phone: 267-702-6760

ISBN: 978-1-7330964-3-0

First Printing: 2024

LEADx® is a registered trademark of LEADx®, Inc., Philadelphia, PA.

Table of Contents

Chapter 1

"THE SLAP HEARD 'ROUND THE WORLD" OR THE NEUROSCIENCE OF EMOTIONS

*"Oh-ho-ho, wow! Wow! Will Smith just smacked the s*** out of me."*
—*Chris Rock*

*"Keep my wife's name out your f******* mouth."*
—*Will Smith*

DEFINITION
Emo·tion
A reaction pattern involving experiential, physiological, and behavioral elements. (Source: American Psychological Association)

RESEARCH
Emotions can be triggered in the *subconscious* in as little as 20 milliseconds. (Schräder et al., 2023, Consciousness and Cognition, 110, 103493)

It was the slap heard around the world.

March 27, 2022, at the 94th Academy Awards. It was supposed to be the greatest night of Will Smith's career. He would go on to win the Best Actor award for his role portraying Serena and Venus Williams' dad in the movie *King Richard*. This was his crowning achievement after decades of roles as the fun, loveable action hero (the good guy!).

But the ceremony took an unexpected turn when comedian Chris Rock took the stage and launched into his monologue. With Will Smith and his wife, Jada Pinkett Smith, seated in the front row, Rock made a joke about Pinkett Smith's shaved head. "Jada, I love you. G.I. Jane 2, can't wait to see it."

At first, Will Smith laughed and clapped once. His wife rolled her eyes, and the crowd groaned. Jada Pinkett Smith suffers from alopecia and experiences hair loss as a side effect.

Smith took the stage, striding purposefully, and proceeded to slap Rock hard across the face. Smith turned around and walked back to his seat with an expression of self-satisfaction and indignation.

Rock's reaction to being assaulted in front of 20 million live viewers was more of a non-reaction. He was so calm that many people thought the whole thing was staged.

"Will Smith just slapped the (expletive) out of me," Rock said evenly.

From his seat, Smith yelled out, "Keep my wife's name out of your f******* mouth."

"Wow, dude. It was a 'G.I. Jane' joke," Rock replied.

Smith screamed again from his seat, louder and with more emphasis, "Keep my wife's name out your f****** mouth!"

Finally, Rock said before moving on, "I'm going to,

okay…That was a…greatest night in the history of television, okay."

Let's put aside any debate about the joke itself—whether it was appropriate or not, whether it crossed any lines related to race, gender, or disease.

The key question is: did that slap help or hurt Will Smith's career? Do you think he wishes he could take it back?

In the aftermath, Smith was banned from the Oscars for ten years. His next movie, *Emancipation*, despite getting great reviews from critics, was considered a flop at the box office. It remains to be seen if he can reclaim the adoration of his fans and the respect of his peers.

Now, you might not be going to the Oscars any time soon. Thankfully, physical altercations at work are incredibly rare. But how might this Chris Rock and Will Smith incident cause you to reflect on how emotions can hijack your behavior and hold you back from being the best version of yourself?

Have you seen any leaders lose their cool and scream, curse, or throw things in the office?

Did it increase the engagement of those on their team or damage it? Did that leader gain or lose respect?

Alternatively, have you seen colleagues who kept their cool under pressure? Who remained composed even in extreme circumstances? Did they lose or earn esteem in these times?

What *Are* Emotions?

Before we discuss emotional intelligence, we have to start with a basic question, "What *are* emotions?"

As psychologist Paul Kleinginna once said, "Everyone knows what an emotion is until asked to give a definition. Then, it seems, no one knows."

On the surface, the question itself seems simple or even silly. We might leap to an answer with examples like "happy, sad, frustrated, excited." Or, in Will Smith's case, angry.

But ever since Charles Darwin wrote *The Expression of the Emotions in Man and Animals* in 1872, scientists have been seeking to understand emotions without much agreement.

Images from Charles Darwin's book The Expression of the Emotions in Man and Animals *which explores the animal origins of human emotions.*

In fact, psychologist Paul Ekman called Darwin's book foundational to the entire field of psychology. In his research on emotions, Ekman proposed that humans experience six basic emotions: anger, fear, surprise, disgust, joy, and sadness. Other scientists claim there are just four basic emotions; still others count 27.

One thing is very clear, though — emotions arise from activity in distinct brain areas. In a gross simplification of neurobiology, here's how you can think about emotions in the brain…

The amygdala is a small area in the center of our brain,

between our ears. Think of this area as our reptilian brain–
the brain that was formed initially in early evolution. This
area is always standing guard and is responsible for our
fight-or-flight response.

If our eyes perceive a saber-toothed tiger, a spider, or
maybe just a mean person at work, the sensory information
goes to a relay station in the brain called the thalamus. The
thalamus then sends the sensory information to the amygdala in the center of our brain, which determines if the information is a threat – and it errs on the side of thinking
things are threatening. After all, better safe than sorry. It's
the amygdala that activates stress hormones like adrenaline
and cortisol to get us ready to fight, flee, or freeze.

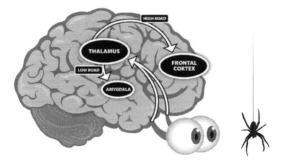

Emotions take the "low road" before they take the "high road."
This means we feel our emotions before we think about them.

Another important brain area is the prefrontal cortex, which regulates our thoughts and actions. It helps us
with impulse control, decision-making, and planning. The
prefrontal cortex is located in the front of our brain, behind our forehead. It developed later in our evolutionary

development. In fact, even today, the prefrontal cortex doesn't fully develop until we're in our mid-twenties.

A key point is that emotions happen non-consciously. Emotions reach the amygdala *before they reach the prefrontal cortex*. This is sometimes called the "low road" in brain processing, which is the more immediate primal pathway.

A common phrase among emotion researchers is, "What is psychological is ultimately biological." This primal low road causes the physical state of an emotion to occur before we realize we have an emotion or the reasons behind it. Emotions trigger physiological responses, impacting heart rate, blood pressure, and perspiration. Often, we display effects on the body through our facial expressions and body language.

Will Smith, for example, heard an insult to his wife and took the low road. He didn't consider his options or take a deep breath. He reacted, and his reaction was literally to "fight."

Given how emotions work, it's important to develop emotional intelligence to help us regulate our emotions and foster positive relationships.

CHAPTER 2

WHAT IS EMOTIONAL INTELLIGENCE?

"It takes something more than intelligence to act intelligently."
—*Fyodor Dostoyevsky*

"People are hired for their skills; they are fired for their behaviors."
—*Unknown*

DEFINITION

emo·tion·al in·tel·li·gence
The ability to recognize, understand, and manage your emotions, as well as recognize and influence the emotions of those around you.

RESEARCH

"Our research shows that emotional intelligence is responsible for 58% of performance in all types of jobs…90% of top performers are high in EQ." —Travis Bradberry, PhD

What Is Emotional Intelligence?

The term "emotional intelligence" was first used in 1990 by researchers John Mayer and Peter Salovey and later popularized by psychologist Daniel Goleman. It is often referred to as EQ or EI.

Emotional intelligence is:

The ability to recognize, understand, and manage your emotions, as well as recognize and influence the emotions of others in a constructive way.

If we unpack that official definition a bit further, emotional intelligence can be broken into four core skills:

- Self-Awareness of your own emotions
- Self-Management of your emotions
- Social Awareness of other people's emotions
- Relationship Management with others

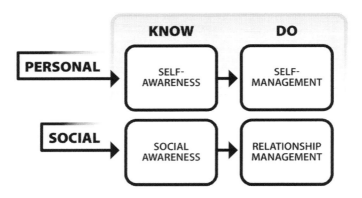

Your EQ is made up of four core skills.

EQ: Self-Awareness

Imagine if you had a clear understanding of the kind of work, people, and experiences that trigger your negative emotions like boredom, frustration, anger, and stress.

And imagine if you knew how to seek out the kind of work, people, and experiences that led to feelings of passion, energy, fulfillment, and joy.

Self-awareness is the foundation of emotional intelligence. It's the skill of peering into your emotional core, recognizing each emotion as it surfaces, and understanding its origin and impact on your actions and decisions. It's understanding why you get flustered in meetings, why compliments make you squirm, and what truly motivates you to chase that next big thing.

Because emotions drive so much of who we are and what we do, having great self-awareness includes awareness of things like:

- Strengths
- Derailers
- Motivations
- Biases

Self-awareness doesn't require years of psychotherapy or a decade-long vow of silence. It simply begins with noticing your feelings as they arise. When you notice a feeling, it gives you the opportunity to *pause*, consider its source, and then decide on a response.

I have a friend who is a Buddhist and a daily meditator, and he's always looking to sharpen the blade of emotional awareness. He told me once that he would use a statement to identify his dominant feeling at any given time. For example, while waiting at the airport for a delayed flight, he might think, "So this is what boredom feels like." Or even when he is feeling down without a known cause, "So this is what mild depression feels like."

My friend taught me that simply acknowledging the negative feeling is often enough to weaken its hold on him.

If he could notice his emotional state, he could also remember that it would inevitably pass. As Zen monk Thich Nhat Hahn wrote, "Feelings come and go like clouds in a windy sky."

The same technique can be used to capture positive emotions, too. While staring at your sleeping child, you may reflect, "So this is what unconditional love feels like." Gazing at a perfect sunset, "This is what awe feels like." Coming out of a period of deep focus on work, "Ahh, this is what being in flow feels like."

Pop Quiz!

How many emotions can you name? Go ahead before you read any further. Just say as many emotions as you can out loud.

How many did you get? Five? Ten? Most people can rattle off the main ones. Anger. Fear. Sadness. Disgust. Love. Happiness. Joy. Frustration. Hate.

Eskimo tribes have dozens of words for snow, and people with high EQ self-awareness usually know dozens of labels for their emotions. This is sometimes called "mining your emotions" (i.e., digging deeper past your surface-level emotions). The richer your emotional vocabulary, the richer your experience of the world becomes, allowing you to communicate feelings more effectively and navigate social interactions with greater ease.

One unique study called "Feelings Into Words: Contributions of Language to Exposure Therapy" investigated how labeling emotions can reduce fear and stress in response to phobias. Specifically, researchers compared groups of people with extreme arachnophobia–a fear of spiders. All groups experienced "exposure therapy," including actually touching a live tarantula, and they were wired up to record their physiologic stress levels (e.g., pulse, perspiration, etc.). However, one group was asked to distract themselves by talking about something unrelated, another was asked to purposely downplay the threat they felt, and the third group was asked to label the emotions they were feeling. It was only this third "labeling your emotions" group that significantly reduced physiological responses and a greater willingness to reapproach the spiders. In fact, the richer the emotional vocabulary used, the more the fear subsided.

There have been many attempts to create a classification system for emotions. One of the most popular systems is Plutchik's Wheel of Emotions, created by psychologist Robert Plutchik in 1980. Since Plutchik created his emotion wheel, many others have followed in his footsteps (like the one pictured here).

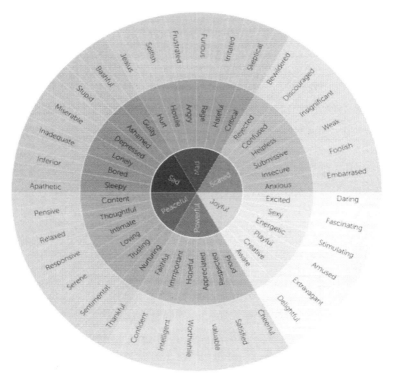

Example emotion wheel which took inspiration from Plutchik.

The idea is to illustrate primary emotions—joy, trust, fear, surprise, sadness, anticipation, anger, and disgust. Around these primary emotions are secondary and tertiary blends that occur from the mixing of the primary emotions, similar to mixing colors on a color wheel.

As an exercise, you can ask yourself, "How do I feel?" Begin at the center of the wheel with the simpler emotional categories and move your way out, getting more and more specific. You should land on a word that best fits how you feel.

We don't have to become fluent in all of Plutchik's named emotions to become masters of emotional self-awareness. It

begins with noticing our feelings–catching them quickly–
so we can then determine what we want to do, if anything,
next.

EQ: Self-Management

The modern workplace is characterized by constant change,
tight deadlines, and interpersonal dynamics that can be emotionally charged. This environment demands individuals
who can manage their emotions effectively. Yet, mastering
self-management doesn't mean suppressing our emotions;
rather, it involves understanding and regulating them, con-
trolling our impulses, and maintaining composure under
stress. With strong self-management skills, we're not just
reacting; we're responding thoughtfully. In short, self-management is about responding to your awareness in the most
constructive way you can. This cultivated ability significantly
enhances several key areas:

- Accountability: We own our actions and outcomes.
- Agility: We adapt swiftly to changing circumstances.
- Resilience: We bounce back from setbacks with strength.
- Decision Making: We make informed choices even in difficult situations.

Consider the Will Smith slap of Chris Rock that we in-
troduced in Chapter One. In anger, Smith leaped onto the
stage and struck Rock. But what else could he have done
instead? He could have:

- Yelled his expletive-filled threat from his seat without physical violence
- Walked out of the event in protest, leaving the Academy in an awkward position since he wouldn't be present to claim the main prize of the night
- Used his acceptance speech to scold the Academy and Rock for bullying people over their medical conditions
- Waited until a commercial break to slap Rock out of the view of the cameras

And, of course, he could have done nothing and stayed in his seat.

We can see that Smith had unlimited options. And if he had had better self-management at that moment, he probably would have chosen a different course of action, one that would not have hurt his career.

As the Holocaust survivor and psychologist Victor Frankl famously said, "Between stimulus and response, there is a space. In that space, it is our power to choose our response."

Self-management is about leveraging that space to choose the best response. For example, when pursuing lofty goals, you will inevitably encounter setbacks and feel frustrated. You might feel like giving up. But will you give up? Or will you push through despite your negative emotions? Giving feedback to team members almost always feels uncomfortable. Nobody likes telling someone they aren't doing good enough. But will you give them hard, constructive feedback, or will you let it fester?

Managing our emotions has the potential to turn inner

chaos into outer calm. It allows us to control our actions and, ultimately, our relationships.

EQ: Social Awareness

In today's multifaceted workplace environment, diversity extends beyond just age, race, and ethnicity—it encompasses a variety of work styles, communication preferences, and cultural backgrounds. Understanding and navigating this complexity is not just beneficial but necessary, and social awareness stands as a critical tool in this endeavor.

Social awareness is the skill that allows us to perceive and understand the emotions, needs, and thoughts of those around us. It enables us to tailor our approach to leadership and interaction, recognizing that each team member is unique. Consider, for instance, how different individuals within the same team might respond to work and communication:

- The Lone Wolves and the Team Players: Which team members flourish in independent work, and which find their energy in collaboration?
- The Change Champions and the Adapters: Who readily embraces new initiatives, and who might require more explanation and support to see the value of a shift?
- The Feedback Seekers and the Sensitive Souls: How can you provide feedback that motivates the high achievers who crave constant improvement while ensuring constructive criticism doesn't dishearten those who need a gentler approach?

Social awareness is a core skill that drives not just empathy, but also awareness of organizational dynamics, politics, and cultural differences. What are the working norms among people of different management levels, or between different departments? What is the standard practice for remote meetings–cameras on, or cameras optional?

Two fundamental tactics in developing strong social awareness are active listening and reading body language. Active listening involves fully engaging with the speaker and understanding their perspective before responding. Reading body language, on the other hand, helps to pick up on unspoken issues or feelings that might not be directly communicated.

Importantly, social awareness is not akin to mind reading. A crucial part of social awareness is to avoid making assumptions based on incomplete information. For example, just because someone is quiet in a meeting doesn't necessarily mean they are bored or disinterested. It also doesn't mean they are in agreement. They might simply be processing the information or hesitant to share their thoughts. A socially aware leader would recognize this and encourage participation, perhaps by saying, "Jean, you've been very quiet. We'd love to hear your thoughts on this topic."

Difficult situations are inevitable in the workplace. When team members underperform or exhibit behavior that conflicts with company values, social awareness empowers you to "get curious, not furious." Instead of resorting to anger, seek to understand the root cause of the behavior. Is there a lack of clarity in expectations? Are they facing personal challenges that are impacting their performance?

Curiosity fosters open communication and paves the way for solutions.

While self-awareness and self-management are foundational aspects of emotional intelligence, it is social awareness that truly enables effective interaction within the complexities of human dynamics at work. By mastering this skill, leaders and professionals can not only enhance their own interpersonal effectiveness but also contribute to a more inclusive, supportive, and productive workplace environment.

EQ: Relationship Management

Relationship management goes beyond mere courtesy or networking. It's the strategic use of your entire EQ arsenal – self-awareness, self-management, and social awareness – to build and maintain healthy relationships with others.

Competencies related to strong relationship management include:

- Trust Building: The bedrock of all relationships, trust is cultivated through consistent, honest interactions and a commitment to integrity.
- Coaching: Far from merely instructing, effective coaching means fostering an environment where others can learn and grow through feedback and support.
- Conflict Management: The inevitability of conflict makes managing it a vital skill, transforming potential breakdowns into breakthroughs.
- Inclusivity: Genuine relationship management embraces diversity, ensuring that inclusivity is woven into the fabric of team dynamics.

- Influence: This involves shaping outcomes and inspiring change, not through authority but through persuasion and example.

While it might be relatively straightforward to manage relationships in the short term, such as during the honeymoon phases of new work assignments, romantic endeavors, or friendships, the real challenge lies in maintaining these relationships over time, especially under stress or fatigue.

The good news is that even small, consistent investments in relationships over time will yield big results. Echoing Stephen Covey's concept from *The 7 Habits of Highly Effective People*, relationships can be likened to emotional bank accounts. Every interaction you have either deposits into or withdraws from this account. Positive behaviors like fulfilling promises, showing kindness, and maintaining honesty contribute to deposits, thereby building a reservoir of goodwill and trust. On the other hand, negative actions such as disrespect or failing to keep one's word act as withdrawals. Maintaining a healthy balance in these accounts is crucial for enduring relationships that can survive occasional conflicts and misunderstandings.

Relationship management is not a peripheral skill; it's a core competency for success in today's workplace. By cultivating empathy, effective communication, and a collaborative spirit, individuals can build strong and lasting relationships. This, in turn, fosters a more positive work environment, enhanced productivity, and, ultimately, a competitive edge in the ever-evolving business landscape.

Chapter #3

HOW TO TAKE THE LEADx EMOTIONAL INTELLIGENCE ASSESSMENT

"If you can't measure it, you can't improve it."
—Peter Drucker

RESEARCH

"Emotional intelligence is not fixed genetically, nor does it develop only in early childhood. Unlike IQ, which changes little after our teen years, research shows that emotional intelligence seems to be largely learned, and it continues to develop as we go through life and learn from our experiences—our competence in it can keep growing."
—Daniel Goleman, PhD

At this point, you might ask, "So, how do I know if I'm emotionally intelligent?"

Better questions to ask yourself are, "What are the areas of EQ where I am *strongest,* and what areas should I focus on for improvement?"

The LEADx EQ-i assessment is designed to give you those answers. It has been rigorously researched and validated by a team of independent psychologists, and it is an accurate measure of your emotional intelligence.

By responding to 40 simple questions, you'll receive a detailed breakdown of your capabilities in each of the four skill areas. You will also be able to receive behavioral nudges and elearning through the LEADx mobile app.

The assessment will categorize your skills into three levels: areas for enrichment, effectively developed skills, and highly enhanced skills. These insights will serve as a reference point that you can return to as you apply the strategies in this book to enhance your emotional intelligence.

LEADx EQ-i: How Do I Take the Test?

To take the LEADx online emotional intelligence test, simply scan the QR code on the front cover, or visit:

www.LEADx.org/free-eq-assessment

Can My Emotional Intelligence Change?

Emotional intelligence is not static—it can indeed change and develop over time. Unlike IQ, which remains relatively fixed throughout one's life, EQ can be improved with targeted efforts. This adaptability stems from EQ's grounding in social and emotional skills, which can be honed through practice, feedback, and learning. The 52 strategies in this book will help you to improve over time. This dynamic quality of EI makes it a valuable focus for personal and professional development.

How Many EQ Skills Should I Try To Improve At the Same Time?

When focusing on improving your emotional intelligence (EQ), it's generally best to start with one or two key areas at a time. Trying to tackle too many EQ skills simultaneously can be overwhelming and may dilute your efforts, making it harder to see tangible progress. Choose a specific skill that aligns closely with your personal or professional goals—such as social awareness if you're looking to enhance your relationships or self-management if you want to manage stress better. By concentrating on one or two areas, you can dedicate enough attention and practice to truly develop these skills before moving on to others.

Is EQ Related to Age or Gender?

Emotional intelligence (EQ) can be influenced by a variety of factors, including age and gender, but these relationships aren't straightforward. Generally, EQ tends to increase as people get older, which is thought to be due to the accumulation of life experiences and a greater emphasis on interpersonal relationships over time. As for gender, some studies suggest that women may, on average, exhibit higher emotional intelligence than men, particularly in areas like empathy and social responsibility. However, these differences are often subtle and heavily influenced by societal, cultural, and individual factors rather than being strictly determined by gender alone. Therefore, while age and gender can have an impact, EQ is largely a skill set that anyone can develop regardless of demographic factors.

How Can Some People Become Highly Successful Even If They Have Low EQ?

Unfortunately, most of us have encountered some senior leader–or even CEO–who seems to have terrible EQ. They may scream or throw tantrums in the face of bad news, they might be tone-deaf to the needs and wishes of their direct reports, and their relationships suffer from distrust. So how did they get promoted all the way up to the role they have now?

Some people achieve high levels of success even with low emotional intelligence through a combination of other strengths or because the culture they are working in favors results at all costs. For instance, individuals with exceptional technical skills, individuals with higher intellectual capacity, and those who are just willing to work 80 hours a week can excel in fields where these attributes are highly valued, even if their interpersonal skills are lacking. Thus, while a high EQ can significantly enhance career and personal life, it's not the sole determinant of success.

SELF-AWARENESS STRATEGIES

By honing your self-awareness, you gain the ability to step back and observe your inner world – your thoughts, feelings, and triggers. This newfound clarity empowers you to make conscious choices, navigate challenging situations effectively, and build stronger relationships.

This chapter will equip you with a toolbox of practical strategies to develop your self-awareness, transforming you from a passive observer of your own life to an active participant in shaping your success.

1. **Journal Your Thoughts and Feelings Daily:** Keep a daily record of your emotions and what triggered them.
2. **Solicit Feedback from People You Trust:** Request constructive feedback from people you trust and review it objectively.
3. **Use Mindfulness Triggers to Check How You're Feeling:** Use cues (like phone alarms and sticky notes) to remind you to check your emotional state.
4. **Reflect on Emotions That Point to Strengths:** To identify your strengths, Journal for 15 minutes each day for a week about when you feel happiest and most engaged.
5. **Reflect on Emotions that Point to Weaknesses:** To identify your weaknesses, spend 15 minutes each day

for a week journaling about when you feel stressed or drained.

6. **Identify and Quash Unconscious Biases:** To uncover your unconscious biases, spend 15 minutes each day for a week journaling about strong reactions or quick judgments.

7. **Identify and Quash Decision Biases:** To uncover decision-making biases, spend 15 minutes each day for a week journaling about significant decisions.

8. **Label Your Emotions with Precision:** Label your feelings accurately to understand their nature and origin; expand your emotional vocabulary.

9. **Perform Regular Body Scans:** Perform daily body scans to check for physical signs of emotional stress or discomfort.

10. **Use In-the-Moment Questioning:** Next time you find yourself in an emotional moment, ask yourself questions like, "Why am I feeling this?"

11. **Hone Your Emotional Listening:** Practice active listening during conversations to better understand your own emotional responses.

12. **Analyze Past Interactions:** Reflect on past social interactions to identify what went well or poorly emotionally for you.

13. **Learn about EQ from the World Around You:** Choose a book, show, movie, or conversation and look at it with emotional intelligence top of mind. Compare your observations to how you might have felt or acted in the same situation.

SA1. Journal Your Thoughts and Feelings Daily

By consistently writing about your thoughts and emotions, you can uncover patterns and triggers in your behavior. This simple practice involves setting aside a few minutes each day to reflect on your experiences and document your emotional responses.

1. Set a Routine: Choose a specific time each day to journal. Morning or evening tends to work best for consistent reflection.
2. Create a Calm Space: Find a quiet, comfortable place where you won't be interrupted.
3. Reflect on Your Day: Think about the events of your day and how they made you feel. Focus on moments that elicited strong emotions.
4. Write Freely: Jot down your thoughts and feelings without censoring yourself. Be honest and detailed.
5. Identify Patterns: After a week, review your entries to identify recurring themes or triggers in your emotional responses.
6. Develop Strategies: Based on your insights, brainstorm ways to manage your emotional triggers more effectively. This could involve improving communication, setting boundaries, or practicing relaxation techniques.
7. Regularly Review: Make it a habit to regularly review and reflect on your journal entries to track your progress and adjust your strategies as needed.

For Managers

As a manager, journaling can enhance your leadership skills by helping you understand your emotional triggers. For example, if you notice yourself feeling frustrated during team meetings, you can explore the reasons behind this emotion in your journal. Reflecting on these moments might reveal that the frustration stems from a lack of preparation among team members. Armed with this insight, you can take proactive steps to break the pattern. You might set clearer expectations for meeting preparations and guidelines for how to engage in each meeting.

For Individual Contributors

For individual contributors, journaling can improve your ability to work effectively with your peers. Suppose you find yourself feeling anxious when receiving critical feedback. By documenting these instances in your journal, you can delve into the root causes of your anxiety. You might discover that it relates to a fear of not meeting expectations or to perfectionism. Recognizing this pattern allows you to reframe feedback sessions as opportunities for growth rather than personal critiques. This shift in perspective can enhance your professional development and collaboration with colleagues.

For Home Life

At home, journaling can strengthen your relationships with family members. As a parent or spouse, documenting your emotional responses can help you navigate challenging situations more effectively. For instance, if you feel overwhelmed by household responsibilities, writing about your feelings of overwhelm can provide clarity. You may realize that it stems from feeling unsupported. This awareness enables you to communicate your needs more effectively to your partner or children, fostering a more cooperative and harmonious home environment.

TAKE ACTION: This week, set aside 10 minutes each day to journal about your thoughts and emotions to enhance your self-awareness.

SA2. Solicit Feedback from People You Trust

Asking others how they view your emotional states is a powerful way to gain deeper self-awareness. This feedback solicitation activity involves regularly seeking input from colleagues, friends, or family members about how you express and manage your emotions. Like watching footage of yourself giving a presentation, other people will offer insights into your behavior that you might be blind to.

How to Do It

1. Identify Key People: Select a few trusted individuals from different areas of your life—work, home, and friends—whose opinions you value.
2. Set Regular Check-Ins: Schedule regular intervals (e.g., monthly or quarterly) to ask for feedback. Consistency is key to gaining accurate insights.
3. Ask Specific Questions: Prepare specific questions about your emotional states. For example, "How do you perceive my emotional responses during stressful situations?"
4. Listen Actively: When receiving feedback, listen without interrupting or defending yourself. Show appreciation for their honesty and insights.
5. Reflect and Act: Reflect on the feedback and identify actionable steps to improve your emotional management. Implement these changes and monitor your progress.
6. Follow Up: After some time, follow up with the same

individuals to see if they have noticed improvements and to gather additional feedback.

For Managers

As a manager, understanding how your team perceives your emotional states is crucial for effective leadership. For example, you might ask your team members for feedback during one-on-one meetings or use an anonymous survey. Suppose you discover that your team perceives you as stressed and unapproachable during high-pressure situations. With this feedback, you can work on developing strategies to manage stress more effectively and project a calm demeanor (e.g., mindfulness techniques or setting aside time for relaxation before critical meetings).

For Individual Contributors

For individual contributors, soliciting feedback on your emotional states can improve your interactions with peers. Imagine asking a colleague for feedback after a project. They might reveal that during tight deadlines, you come across as tense and hurried, which affects team morale. Recognizing this, you can focus on improving your stress management techniques, such as breaking tasks into smaller steps or taking short breaks to reset.

For Home Life

At home, asking family members for feedback on your emotional states can strengthen your relationships. As a parent or spouse, you might discover that your partner feels you are often irritable after work. Understanding this perception can help you take proactive steps to manage your emotions before engaging with your family. For instance, you could establish a routine of unwinding for a few minutes after arriving home or practicing deep breathing exercises.

TAKE ACTION: This week, ask at least one trusted person for feedback on how they perceive your emotional state and implement their suggestions.

SA3. Use Mindfulness Triggers to Check How You're Feeling

A potent tool to enrich your self-awareness is the use of mindfulness triggers—specific cues that prompt you to engage in mindful reflection about your current state of being. Whether it's setting a reminder on your phone or a physical object, these triggers can prompt you to self-reflect throughout the day.

How to Do It

1. Identify Key Moments: Choose significant instances in your day when a mindfulness check-in would be beneficial.

2. Select Your Triggers: Pick cues that will serve as your triggers. These can be anything from alarms to visual tokens.

3. React to the Trigger: When the trigger occurs, take a minute to pause, breathe, and reflect on your current emotional state.

4. Journal the Experience: Make a quick note of your emotional state and any significant insights you gain during the pause.

5. Calibrate: Based on your journal entries, adjust your triggers or your reactions to them for better effectiveness.

6. Review and Reflect: Periodically review your journal to identify patterns in your emotional states or reactions to similar situations.

For Managers

If you're a manager, a mindfulness trigger can help you come across as more thoughtful and caring. For example, a trigger could remind you to gauge your stress level before stepping into a team meeting. This mindful pause allows you time to make adjustments. You might take a few deep breaths or rephrase your intended message.

For Individual Contributors

If you're an individual contributor, mindfulness triggers can help you better navigate your interpersonal dynamics in collaborative environments. For instance, a trigger could prompt you to reflect on your emotional state before giving feedback to a colleague. This can help you avoid mistakes like giving overly harsh feedback in a bad mood or overly positive feedback in a good mood.

For Home Life

At home, mindfulness triggers can greatly benefit intimate relationships. A trigger could be as simple as a sticky note on your bathroom mirror reminding you to check in with your emotional state before discussing plans for the day with your spouse or children. This simple pause can help you slow down, go into your discussion with a clear head, and facilitate better communication.

TAKE ACTION: This week, identify three key moments—one at work, one with your team, and one at home—to set mindfulness triggers. Follow through and journal your insights.

SA4. Reflect on Emotions That Point to Strengths

Reflecting on your happiest moments or those times when you're completely absorbed in an activity—known as a flow state—can reveal the types of roles and tasks you naturally excel in. This simple journaling exercise can help you identify your strengths and better align your career and personal life with your inherent talents.

How to Do It

1. Set Aside Time: Dedicate at least 15 minutes a day for one week to reflect on your activities.
2. Identify Peak Moments: Write down the times when you felt happiest, most engaged, or in a flow state.
3. Analyze the Activities: Look for common themes or tasks that consistently bring you joy and satisfaction.
4. Reflect on Emotions: Note any negative feelings and the activities associated with them.
5. Make Connections: Identify how these activities relate to your roles at work and home.
6. Set Goals: Determine how you can incorporate more of these positive activities into your daily routine.
7. Review and Adjust: Regularly revisit your journal to refine your understanding of your strengths and adjust your activities accordingly.

For Managers

As a manager, understanding your strengths is crucial. Spend time reflecting on the moments at work when you felt most engaged and effective. For example, you might notice that leading brainstorming sessions brings you joy and energizes your team. Conversely, you may feel drained after handling administrative tasks. By recognizing these patterns, you can delegate more effectively and focus on activities that leverage your leadership strengths.

For Individual Contributors

For individual contributors, this exercise can improve collaboration and job satisfaction. Reflect on interactions with peers and projects that left you feeling accomplished. Perhaps you thrive when working on creative tasks or find satisfaction in solving complex problems. Identifying these strengths can help you seek out projects that align with your skills, leading to better performance and increased job fulfillment. For instance, if you realize you're happiest when collaborating on innovative projects, you can volunteer for roles that require creativity and teamwork.

For Home Life

At home, this journaling exercise can enhance your relationships. Reflect on the moments when you felt most connected and effective as a parent or spouse. You might discover that you feel happiest during family game nights or when helping your children with their homework. Conversely, you may find that certain routines or chores are a source of frustration. By understanding these patterns, you can work with your family to distribute tasks more equitably and focus on activities that strengthen your bonds and bring joy to your household.

TAKE ACTION: This week, spend 15 minutes each day journaling about when you feel happiest and most engaged to identify your strengths.

SA5. Reflect on Emotions that Point to Weaknesses

Reflecting on the moments when you feel unhappy, stressed, or drained of energy can reveal the activities and roles that may not be suited to your strengths. This simple journaling exercise can help you identify your weaknesses or derailers, allowing you to make more informed decisions about your career and personal life.

How to Do It

1. Set Aside Time: Dedicate at least 15 minutes a day for one week to reflect on your activities.
2. Identify Low Points: Write down the times when you felt unhappy, stressed, or drained.
3. Analyze the Activities: Look for common themes or tasks that consistently bring you negative emotions.
4. Reflect on Emotions: Note any positive feelings and the activities associated with them for contrast.
5. Make Connections: Identify how these negative activities relate to your roles at work and home.
6. Set Goals: Determine how you can minimize or delegate these negative activities.
7. Review and Adjust: Regularly revisit your journal to refine your understanding of your weaknesses and adjust your activities accordingly.

For Managers

As a manager, it's crucial to recognize the tasks and situations that lead to stress or dissatisfaction. Spend time reflecting on the aspects of your role that leave you feeling depleted. For instance, you might notice that handling conflict resolution drains you, whereas strategic planning invigorates you. By identifying your patterns, you can delegate tasks that are not your strengths and focus on what energizes you. This not only enhances your effectiveness but also boosts the overall morale of your team.

For Individual Contributors

For individual contributors, this exercise can highlight areas where you might need support or development. Reflect on your daily tasks and interactions with peers, noting when you feel most stressed or disengaged. For example, you might find that detailed data analysis is a source of frustration, while collaborative projects excite you. Recognizing your weaknesses allows you to seek help, improve skills, or shift your focus to areas where you can excel and contribute more effectively to your team.

For Home Life

At home, understanding your derailers can improve your family dynamics. Reflect on the activities that leave you feeling drained and how they impact your interactions with loved ones. You might discover that certain routines, such as managing household finances, are a significant source of stress. By acknowledging these weaknesses, you can discuss with your spouse or family members about redistributing these tasks, leading to a more harmonious home environment and better relationships.

TAKE ACTION: This week, spend 15 minutes each day journaling about when you feel stressed or drained to identify your weaknesses.

SA6. Identify and Quash Unconscious Biases

Reflecting on your daily interactions and reactions can uncover unconscious biases, helping you become more self-aware. This journaling exercise involves recording and analyzing moments when you felt a strong emotional reaction or made a quick judgment, aiming to identify hidden biases such as affinity bias, appearance bias, age bias, and gender bias that influence your behavior.

How to Do It

1. Set Aside Time: Dedicate at least 15 minutes a day for one week to reflect on your interactions.
2. Identify Biases You've Let Affect You: Don't judge yourself or feel guilty. This is how you learn!
3. Recall Specific Behaviors: Try to remember specific moments when these biases affected your thinking or actions.
4. Reflect on Patterns: Did any biases come up more than once? Consider how these patterns might indicate underlying biases, such as affinity, appearance, age, or gender biases.
5. Make Connections: Identify how these biases affect your roles at work and at home.
6. Set Goals: Determine how you can address and mitigate these biases in your daily interactions.
7. Review and Adjust: Regularly revisit your journal to refine your understanding of your biases and adjust your behavior accordingly.

For Managers

As a manager, uncovering unconscious biases is crucial for more caring and inclusive leadership. Spend time reflecting on your interactions with team members, especially those that elicited strong reactions. For example, you might notice a pattern of affinity bias, favoring team members who share your interests or background during brainstorming sessions. By recognizing this bias, you can make a conscious effort to involve everyone equally, fostering a more inclusive and innovative team environment.

For Individual Contributors

For individual contributors, this exercise can improve collaboration and personal growth. Reflect on your interactions with colleagues and note any instances where you felt judgmental or had an automatic reaction. For instance, if you realize you have an age bias, favoring younger colleagues for tech-related tasks, you can consciously work on valuing the diverse experiences of all team members, regardless of age. Recognizing these biases allows you to approach collaborations with a more open mind, improving teamwork and reducing conflicts.

For Home Life

At home, understanding and addressing unconscious biases can strengthen your relationships. Reflect on interactions with your spouse or children, especially those that led to conflicts or misunderstandings. You might find that certain biases, such as gender roles, influence your behavior. For example, if you realize you unconsciously expect your spouse to handle certain chores based on gender, discussing and redistributing these tasks can lead to a more balanced and harmonious household. Additionally, being aware of any age bias towards your children can help you better understand and respect their viewpoints and capabilities. Acknowledging these biases enables you to communicate more openly and equitably with your family.

TAKE ACTION: This week, spend 15 minutes each day journaling about strong reactions or quick judgments to uncover unconscious biases.

SA7. Identify and Quash Decision Biases

Reflecting on your decision-making process can help you uncover biases that may impact your judgment. This journaling exercise involves recording and analyzing decisions you've made, focusing on the rationale behind them, and identifying potential biases such as recency bias, the bandwagon effect, and anchoring bias.

How to Do It

1. Set Aside Time: Dedicate at least 15 minutes a day for one week to reflect on your decisions.
2. Identify Key Decisions: Write down significant decisions and the context in which they were made.
3. Read Through the List of Biases in the Table at the End of This Strategy: Skim through the names and definitions.
4. Mark Any that You've Let Affect Key Decisions: Don't judge yourself or feel guilty. This is how you learn!
5. Reflect on Patterns: Did any biases come up more than once? Consider how these patterns might indicate underlying biases, such as affinity, appearance, age, or gender biases.
6. Make Connections: Identify how these biases affect your decisions.
7. Set Goals: Determine how you can address and mitigate these biases in future decisions.
8. Review and Adjust: Regularly revisit your journal to refine your understanding of your decision biases and adjust your behavior accordingly.

For Managers

As a manager, recognizing decision-making biases can help you improve the decisions that impact your team. Spend time reflecting on significant decisions you've made and the factors that influenced them. For instance, you might notice a recency bias, where recent events or performances heavily influence your evaluations and decisions. This bias can lead to unfair assessments of team members based on recent successes or failures rather than overall performance. By identifying this pattern, you can take a more balanced approach, ensuring fair and comprehensive evaluations.

For Individual Contributors

For individual contributors, this exercise can help you critically assess group decisions and voice your unique perspective, contributing to more robust and well-rounded outcomes. Reflect on decisions made during projects and interactions with colleagues. You might discover the bandwagon effect, where you tend to agree with the majority's opinion to avoid conflict or standing out. You may also realize that you often conform to team opinions without fully expressing your ideas. Equipped with awareness, you can work on building the confidence you need to share your differing viewpoints.

For Home Life

At home, understanding and addressing decision-making biases can improve how you make important family decisions. Reflect on family decisions, such as financial planning or parenting strategies, and consider the factors that influenced these choices. You might find that anchoring bias, where the first piece of information you received overly influenced your decision, played a role in how you prepare meals for your kids. Acknowledging this bias enables you to seek out diverse perspectives and information, leading to more informed and balanced meal choices.

Bias Name	Definition	How to Recognize This Bias in Your Own Thinking and Actions
Confirmation Bias	The tendency to search for, interpret, and remember information in a way that confirms one's preconceptions.	Notice if you are only seeking out information that confirms what you already believe and ignoring contradictory evidence.
Anchoring Bias	The tendency to rely too heavily on the first piece of information encountered when making decisions.	Be aware if you are fixating on an initial piece of information and not considering subsequent information equally.
Availability Heuristic	A mental shortcut that relies on immediate examples that come to mind.	Check if you are making judgments based on the most readily available information rather than all relevant information.
Bandwagon Effect	The tendency to do or believe things because many other people do or believe the same.	Consider if you are adopting beliefs or behaviors just because others around you are doing the same.
Self-Serving Bias	The tendency to attribute positive events to one's own character but attribute negative events to external factors.	Reflect on whether you are taking credit for successes but blaming outside factors for failures.

Bias Name	Definition	How to Recognize This Bias in Your Own Thinking and Actions
Hindsight Bias	The inclination to see events as having been predictable after they have already occurred.	Observe if you are thinking, 'I knew it all along' after an event has occurred despite not predicting it beforehand.
Representative Bias	The tendency to judge the probability of an event by how much it resembles a typical case.	Assess if you are assuming something is likely because it matches a stereotype or typical example.
Overconfidence Bias	The tendency to be more confident in one's abilities than is objectively warranted.	Evaluate whether your confidence in your decisions and abilities is disproportionately high compared to the evidence.
Recency Bias	The tendency to weigh recent events more heavily than earlier events.	Think about whether you are giving disproportionate importance to recent events in your decision-making.
Sunk Cost Fallacy	The decision to continue an investment is based on past investments of time, money, or effort despite new evidence suggesting that the decision was probably wrong.	Consider if you are continuing a course of action because of the time or resources already invested rather than its current merits.
Halo Effect	The tendency to let the overall impression of a person influence specific judgments about them.	Be mindful if a positive impression of someone is leading you to overlook their faults.

Bias Name	Definition	How to Recognize This Bias in Your Own Thinking and Actions
Horns Effect	The tendency to let a single negative trait or action affect one's perception of a person's other traits or actions.	Notice if a negative trait or action of someone is unduly influencing your overall perception of them.
In-Group Bias	The tendency to favor one's own group over others.	Check if you are giving preferential treatment to those who are similar to you.
Out-Group Homogeneity Bias	The perception is that members of an out-group are more similar to each other than are members of one's in-group.	Reflect on whether you are perceiving members of another group as all being alike.
Status Quo Bias	The preference for the current state of affairs and resistance to change.	Observe if you are resistant to change just because you prefer things to stay the same.
Optimism Bias	The tendency to overestimate the likelihood of positive outcomes.	Evaluate whether you are unrealistically expecting positive outcomes.
Pessimism Bias	The tendency to overestimate the likelihood of negative outcomes.	Consider if you are unrealistically expecting negative outcomes.
Gambler's Fallacy	The belief that past events affect the likelihood of something happening in the future in a game of chance.	Notice if you believe a random event is less likely to occur because it happened recently.

Bias Name	Definition	How to Recognize This Bias in Your Own Thinking and Actions
Negativity Bias	The tendency to give more weight to negative experiences or information than positive.	Reflect on whether you are paying more attention to negative information or experiences than positive ones.
Fundamental Attribution Error	The tendency to overemphasize personal characteristics and ignore situational factors in judging others' behavior.	Be aware if you are blaming someone's behavior on their character rather than considering situational factors.
Illusory Correlation	The tendency to see a relationship between two variables when no such relationship exists.	Be aware if you are linking events or variables together without strong evidence.
False Consensus Effect	The tendency to overestimate how much other people agree with one's own beliefs, behaviors, and attitudes.	Notice if you assume others share your views more than they actually do.
Just-World Hypothesis	The belief that the world is just and people get what they deserve.	Reflect on whether you believe that good things happen to good people and bad things happen to bad people.
Framing Effect	The way information is presented affects decisions and judgments.	Observe if the way information is presented is swaying your decisions.
Egocentric Bias	The tendency to rely too heavily on one's own perspective and experiences.	Check if you are overvaluing your own perspective compared to others.

Bias Name	Definition	How to Recognize This Bias in Your Own Thinking and Actions
Belief Bias	The tendency to judge the strength of arguments based on the plausibility of their conclusion.	Assess if you are judging arguments based on how believable their conclusion seems rather than the evidence.
Clustering Illusion	The tendency to see patterns in random events.	Consider if you are seeing patterns in random data or events.
Endowment Effect	The tendency to value something more highly simply because you own it.	Reflect on whether you are placing higher value on items just because they belong to you.
Planning Fallacy	The tendency to underestimate how long it will take to complete a task.	Evaluate if you are consistently underestimating the time needed to complete tasks.
Outcome Bias	The tendency to judge a decision based on its outcome rather than on the quality of the decision at the time it was made.	Notice if you are judging past decisions based on their outcomes rather than the decision process.

TAKE ACTION: This week, spend 15 minutes each day journaling about significant decisions to uncover and address decision-making biases.

SA8. Label Your Emotions with Precision

Recognizing and naming your emotions as they occur can significantly enhance your self-awareness. This activity involves consciously pausing to identify your feelings. By accurately labeling your emotions, you can better understand your reactions and manage them effectively. As you expand your emotional vocabulary, you will be able to get more granular about what exactly you're feeling and why.

How to Do It

1. Pause and Reflect: Next time you notice a strong emotion, pause and reflect on what you're feeling.
2. Consider the Cause: Think about what might have triggered this emotion. Understanding the cause provides valuable insights into what exactly you're feeling.
3. Name the Emotion: Clearly identify and name the emotion you are experiencing. Work your way from the middle of the wheel (at the end of this strategy) to the outside. This will help you find a more specific term to describe your feelings.
4. Acknowledge the Emotion: Accept the emotion without judgment. Emotions aren't "good" or "bad." They're biological!
5. Review Regularly: Make it a habit to review and reflect on your emotions regularly to identify patterns.

For Managers

For managers, this practice can help you take proactive measures to create a more organized and supportive work environment for your team. Imagine feeling stressed about an upcoming deadline. By pausing to identify and label your feelings—perhaps recognizing stress, anxiety, and a sense of urgency—you gain clarity on your emotional state. This awareness allows you to address these feelings constructively. For instance, realizing that your stress is due to insufficient resources might prompt you to delegate tasks more efficiently or communicate your concerns to your team.

For Individual Contributors

As an individual contributor, expanding your emotional vocabulary can help you improve your interactions with colleagues. Suppose you feel slighted after a meeting where your suggestions were overlooked. Identifying specific emotions like frustration, disappointment, or feeling undervalued helps you understand your reaction better. With this clarity, you can take constructive steps. You might seek feedback on your ideas or find more effective ways to communicate in meetings.

For Home Life

At home, emotion labeling can strengthen your relationships with family members by reducing tension and increasing understanding of the family dynamic. For example, if you feel overwhelmed by household responsibilities, taking a moment to identify your emotions—such as irritated, exhausted, or unsupported—can help you communicate more effectively with your spouse or children. Expressing these feelings can lead to more productive conversations about sharing responsibilities and providing mutual support.

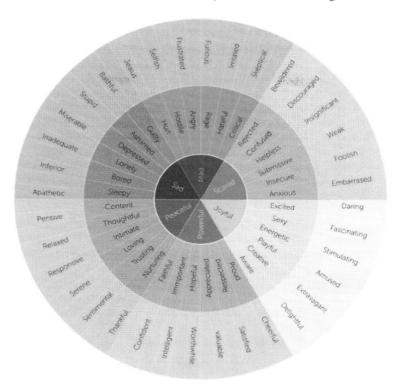

Move your way from the basic emotions at the center of the wheel to the more specific emotions at the outer portion of the wheel. Stop at the emotion that most accurately describes the way you feel.

TAKE ACTION: This week, expand your emotional vocabulary by identifying and labeling your emotions as they occur.

SA9. Perform Regular Body Scans

Psychologist Bessel van der Kolk famously said, "The body keeps the score." The idea is that even if we're not aware of our feelings or trauma, our body is. The body scan is a mindfulness exercise that involves focusing attention on different parts of your body. As you tune into any physical sensations or tensions, you can reveal underlying emotions. Regular body scans will help you enhance your awareness of how emotions manifest physically, allowing you to address them more quickly and effectively.

How to Do It

1. Pause and Breathe: Throughout your day, take a moment to pause and take a few deep breaths.
2. Check In with Your Body: Quickly scan your body from head to toe, noticing any areas of tension or discomfort.
3. Focus on Key Areas: Pay special attention to common areas where tension builds, such as your neck, shoulders, and back.
4. Acknowledge Sensations: Observe any sensations without judgment. Recognize if you're holding tension or experiencing discomfort.
5. Breathe into Tension: Take a deep breath and focus on relaxing any tense areas as you exhale.
6. Adjust Your Posture: Make small adjustments to your posture to alleviate discomfort and improve alignment.
7. Repeat as Needed: Perform this quick body scan

periodically throughout your day, especially during or after stressful moments.

For Managers

For managers, the body scan can be a valuable tool in maintaining a calm and focused leadership style. Imagine facing a high-pressure meeting. By taking a few minutes before the meeting to perform a body scan, you can identify areas of tension and stress. For example, noticing tightness in your shoulders or shallow breathing can signal anxiety. Acknowledging these physical cues allows you to take steps to relax, such as deep breathing or stretching, leading to a more composed and effective presence during the meeting. This practice not only improves your own well-being but also sets a positive tone for your team.

For Individual Contributors

As an individual contributor, using the body scan can improve your well-being and productivity. Suppose you feel distracted and irritable after completing an arduous list of tasks. You might take a moment to perform a body scan, which reveals a clenched jaw and a stiff neck. You recognize these as physical signs of accumulated stress, which prompts you to take a short break and stretch. By addressing your physical and emotional state, you can return to your work with renewed focus and a more positive attitude.

For Home Life

At home, the body scan can be particularly beneficial in managing personal stress. For instance, you might notice a headache and stomach tension, which you know is the result of frustration and worry after your teenager stayed out two hours later than agreed. Once you're aware, you can practice the self-care you need to keep your frustration and worry from hijacking your day.

TAKE ACTION: This week, pause periodically to perform a quick body scan and release tension, enhancing your self-awareness and stress management.

SA10. Use In-The-Moment Question-ing

The In-The-Moment Questioning strategy involves pausing during emotional moments to ask yourself questions like "Why am I feeling this?" This simple yet powerful technique helps you understand your emotions and react more thoughtfully.

How to Do It

1. Pause: When you notice a strong emotion, take a moment to pause. This interruption in your immediate reaction is crucial.
2. Identify the Emotion: Ask yourself, "What am I feeling right now?" Naming the emotion helps in acknowledging it.
3. Question the Why: Follow up with, "Why am I feeling this?" This step helps uncover the underlying reasons behind a strong emotion.
4. Reflect: Consider if the emotion is proportionate to the situation. Reflect on past experiences that might be influencing your current feelings.
5. Respond Thoughtfully: With this understanding, choose a thoughtful response rather than reacting impulsively.

For Managers

As a manager, in-the-moment questioning can help you tune into your emotions more quickly and more deeply. In turn, this will help you come across as more self-assured and thoughtful, and less reactive or impulsive. Imagine receiving unexpected negative feedback during a team meeting. Instead of reacting defensively, take a moment to ask, "Why am I feeling this?" This pause allows you to identify feelings of disappointment or frustration and address them constructively. By understanding your disappointment and frustration, you can respond calmly and foster a more supportive, open environment where team members feel heard and valued.

For Individual Contributors

For individual contributors, this activity can help you receive feedback better. Suppose you're feeling irritated by a colleague's critique of your contribution to a project. Before responding, ask yourself, "Why am I feeling this?" Recognizing that the irritation stems from a fear of inadequacy can help you address the feedback objectively. This self-awareness enables you to engage in productive discussions and strengthens team morale as your team will feel more comfortable offering you feedback in the future.

For Home Life

At home, the In-The-Moment Questioning Activity can help you build a more supportive and understanding family dynamic. Consider a situation where you're feeling overwhelmed by household responsibilities. Instead of snapping at your partner, pause and ask, "Why am I feeling this?" Realizing that the frustration is due to feeling unappreciated can lead to a calm conversation about recognition and sharing duties.

TAKE ACTION: This week, pause and ask yourself, "Why am I feeling this?" whenever you experience a strong emotion.

SA11. Hone Your Emotional Listening

Emotional listening involves using active listening techniques to notice how you're feeling in response to what's being said. This approach helps you become more aware of your emotions and better understand the dynamics of your interactions.

How to Do It

1. Set Your Intention: Before engaging in a conversation, decide to practice emotional listening. Remind yourself to focus on both the speaker's words and your emotional responses.

2. Listen Actively: Pay full attention to the speaker. Use active listening techniques like nodding, summarizing, and asking clarifying questions.

3. Notice Your Emotions: As the conversation progresses, periodically check in with yourself. Ask, "What am I feeling right now?" Name the emotion.

4. Acknowledge Your Feelings: Accept your emotions without judgment. Understanding that all feelings are valid helps you manage them effectively.

5. Reflect and Respond: Use your awareness to guide your response. Aim to respond in a way that is both authentic and constructive.

For Managers

For managers, emotional listening is a powerful tool for fostering open and supportive dialogue. Imagine a team member comes to you with concerns about a project. As you listen, pay attention to your own emotional responses. Are you feeling defensive, empathetic, judgmental, or frustrated? By recognizing these emotions, you can manage your reactions and respond more thoughtfully. For instance, if you notice frustration, you can take a deep breath and focus on understanding the team member's perspective.

For Individual Contributors

As an individual contributor, practicing emotional listening can strengthen your professional relationships. Suppose a colleague criticizes your work in a meeting. Instead of immediately reacting, notice your emotional response. Are you feeling anxious, angry, or embarrassed? Understanding these feelings can help you respond more constructively. You might realize that your anxiety is driving your reaction, allowing you to address the feedback calmly and improve your work.

For Home Life

At home, emotional listening can lead to more harmonious interactions with your spouse or children. Consider a scenario where your partner is expressing frustration about household chores. As you listen, tune into your emotions. Are you feeling overwhelmed, guilty, or defensive? Recognizing these feelings can help you respond more empathetically. If you notice defensiveness, for example, you can focus on validating your partner's feelings and working together to find a solution.

TAKE ACTION: This week, practice emotional listening in at least one conversation and notice your emotional responses.

SA12. Analyze Past Interactions

This strategy helps you understand your emotional triggers and responses. Recall emotionally charged situations from the past, both positive and negative, and reflect on what specifically triggered your emotions and why you felt the way you did.

How to Do It

1. Recall an Interaction: Think back to a specific emotionally charged situation, either positive or negative.
2. Identify the Emotion: Name the primary emotion you felt during the interaction.
3. Pinpoint the Trigger: Reflect on what specifically triggered this emotion. Was it something someone said or did? A specific situation or event?
4. Understand the Why: Dig deeper into why this trigger caused the emotion. Consider past experiences, personal values, or expectations that might influence your feelings.
5. Reflect on Patterns: Look for patterns in your emotional triggers across different situations. Understanding these patterns can help you manage your emotions more effectively in the future.

For Managers

For managers, this activity can be particularly enlightening as a tool to enhance team morale and productivity. Think back to a time when you felt either frustrated or elated by a team member's performance. Perhaps you felt immense satisfaction when a project was completed ahead of schedule.

Reflect on what triggered that positive emotion. Was it the team member's initiative, their problem-solving skills, or the way they communicated progress? By understanding these triggers, you can foster a work environment that encourages behaviors leading to positive emotions and discourages behaviors leading to negative emotions.

For Individual Contributors

As an individual contributor, analyzing past interactions can help you be more proactive about positive behaviors that enhance your productivity. Recall a situation where you felt undervalued during a team meeting. Reflect on why you felt this way. Was it due to a lack of recognition from your peers, or perhaps you felt that your ideas weren't considered? Identifying these triggers can help you address similar situations more constructively in the future. For example, you might decide to voice your ideas more assertively or seek feedback directly.

For Home Life

At home, this activity can help you communicate your needs and foster a supportive and understanding environment. Reflect on a time when you felt particularly close to your spouse during a family event or conversely, a time when you felt disconnected. Analyze what triggered these emotions. Was it the way your spouse supported you in front of your family or perhaps a perceived lack of attention? Understanding these triggers, you might communicate to your spouse how good it made you feel when they supported you in front of the family or how bad it made you feel when you felt like they weren't paying any attention to you.

TAKE ACTION: This week, reflect on one past interaction and analyze what triggered your emotions and why.

SA13. Learn about EQ from the World Around You

While most of the strategies in the self-awareness section of this book have focused on turning inward to understand our emotions, this one turns outward. By looking for examples of emotional intelligence in the world around you, you will grow your awareness of yourself. As you evaluate a fictional character's EQ, and compare your own thoughts and actions to that fictional character, you will grow your self-awareness.

How to Do It

1. Choose Your Medium: Decide whether you want to start with books, movies, shows, or even conversations with friends.

2. Select a Resource: Pick a specific book, movie, show, or video series. Look for recommendations or reviews to ensure it's a good fit.

3. Engage Actively: As you read, watch, or listen, actively think about the emotional dynamics and behaviors presented. Take notes if helpful.

4. Reflect on Learnings: After engaging with the resource, reflect on what you've learned about yourself, your tendencies, and your values, emotions, and behaviors. Consider how these insights apply to your own experiences.

5. Apply the Insights: Use your new understanding to approach your interactions differently. Try out new strategies in your role as a manager, team member, or family member.

6. Continue the Cycle: Make ongoing education a

regular part of your routine. Continuously seek out new resources to deepen your emotional awareness.

For Managers

As a manager, the ongoing education exercise can offer you valuable insights into leadership skills like motivation, persuasion, and values-based leadership. For example, you might watch a show like *Ted Lasso*, where the main character, Coach Ted, has a way of motivating everyone around him. As you watch Ted finally break through to his young, egotistical talent, Jamie, you might pick up on the questions he asks, the body language he uses, and the relationship-building tactics he uses to win Jamie's trust and respect. By getting curious about Ted's approach and comparing it to your own experience as a leader, you can grow your awareness of how you come across to your team.

For Individual Contributors

As an individual contributor, the ongoing education exercise can help you reflect on your own tendencies, values, and style as a team member and colleague. For example, you might watch a contestant on *The Bachelor* get into a pointless, egotistical argument with another contestant. After you've had a good laugh, you might take a second to run the interaction through an EQ lens. Why do you think that happened? How might you navigate that conflict differently if it were you? As you compare this conflict to your own life, you'll build your understanding of yourself, your values, and how you approach conflict.

For Home Life

At home, ongoing education can help you understand how you come across to your spouse and kids and what values you want to bring into your home. For example, as your spouse rehashes a bizarre social interaction he had at the park last week, you might run it through the EQ framework. How would you have navigated the same conversation? Would you do it differently or the same? Why? As you answer this question, you'll begin to grow your understanding of yourself and your tendencies.

TAKE ACTION: This week, choose one book, show, conversation, or movie and reflect on its insights. Compare your insights to how you might have felt or acted had you been in the same situation.

SELF-MANAGEMENT STRATEGIES

In the whirlwind of daily life, it's easy to get swept away by emotions. However, the ability to manage your emotions, rather than be ruled by them, is the key to staying calm under pressure, responding thoughtfully rather than reacting impulsively, and maintaining a positive outlook even in challenging circumstances.

This chapter offers practical tools and techniques to help you gain control of your emotional responses, navigate challenging situations with grace, and ultimately, thrive in all areas of your life.

1. **Set Clear Goals and Review Progress Consistently:** Choose a daily goal and check your progress three times a day to enhance your personal accountability.
2. **Identify the Bright Side of Change:** Develop agility and adaptability by analyzing unexpected changes in your past that led to positive outcomes.
3. **Focus on the Mission:** Identify and focus on your mission, purpose, and goals for increased resilience.
4. **Use a Decision-Making Matrix:** Create a decision matrix for a challenging decision to see how it improves your outcome.
5. **Reframe Negative Situations:** Challenge yourself to reframe negative situations in a more positive light.
6. **Replace Unhelpful Thoughts with Cognitive**

Restructuring: Challenge irrational thoughts that fuel negative emotions.

7. **Control Impulses with Stop-Think-Act:** Practice the Stop-Think-Act approach at least once per day to enhance your self-management skills and improve your reactions in challenging situations.

8. **Use Box Breathing to Manage Stress:** Use this mindfulness exercise to focus on the present moment rather than dwelling on emotional triggers.

9. **Take a Systematic Approach to Problem Solving:** Rather than reacting emotionally, apply a problem-solving approach to conflicts.

10. **Interrupt Negative Thoughts with Thought-Stopping:** Use this cognitive behavioral technique to halt rumination and obsessive thoughts.

11. **Pre-Commit to Bind Yourself to Important Actions:** Make commitments in advance to guide future emotional choices (e.g., "I won't respond to work emails after 9 p.m.").

12. **Define and Set Clear Boundaries:** Learn the art of setting and protecting boundaries to enhance your emotional well-being.

13. **Practice Gratitude:** Take a few minutes each day to reflect on what you're grateful for and observe the impact on your mood and relationships.

SM1. Set Clear Goals and Review Progress Consistently

The Goal Focus Activity involves setting a clear, measurable goal for the day, week, or month and consistently reviewing your progress toward achieving it. This self-management exercise will improve your time management and focus; it will help you to stay on track, even if unpleasant emotions (e.g., stress or boredom) are telling you that you don't want to work on the related tasks.

How to Do It:
1. Set Your Goal: At the beginning of your day, choose one clear, specific, and achievable goal.
2. Write It Down: Note your goal in a place where you can easily see it throughout the day.
3. Check In Regularly: Set reminders to review your progress at least three times during the day.
4. Reflect on Progress: At each check-in, assess how well you are sticking to your goal and make any necessary adjustments.
5. End of Day Review: At the end of the day, reflect on your progress, celebrate successes, and identify areas for improvement.
6. Consider a similar process for your weekly goals.

For Managers
For leaders, begin each day by reviewing your overall team goal and then set a "most important task" for the day. This activity helps keep your management activities aligned with your objectives and can help mitigate feelings of frustration

or overwhelm by providing a clear focus. It will also help you to hold team members accountable for their goals and keep them aligned with the greater purpose.

For Individual Contributors

For team members or individual contributors, it's crucial to align your daily goals with the team's overall objectives to ensure collective success. Start by setting a clear, specific task for the day that directly supports your team's goals. Throughout the day, review this goal and cross-reference it with the team's deadlines and milestones. This practice keeps you focused and productive, preventing any single task from falling behind and potentially jeopardizing the entire project timeline. For instance, if your team is working on a tight deadline for a product launch, ensure your daily contributions are timely and in sync with the broader schedule. By staying aligned and proactive, you help maintain the team's momentum and avoid delays that could impact the overall success.

For Home Life

At home, whether as a parent or a spouse, the Goal Focus Activity can improve relationships and daily interactions. Start your day by setting a goal, like spending quality time with your children or improving communication with your partner. Check in with yourself periodically to see if you're making strides toward this objective. For example, if your goal is to make it home in time for dinner and to go out on a weekly "date night," you can reflect on these personal commitments to make sure your work obligations don't interfere.

TAKE ACTION: This week, choose one daily goal and check your progress three times a day to enhance your personal accountability.

SM2. Identify The Bright Side of Change

Reflecting on past experiences can reveal moments when unexpected changes, initially met with resistance or negative emotions, ultimately led to positive outcomes. Recalling these moments helps to build a mindset that embraces change, fostering agility and adaptability.

How to Do It:

1. Identify the Change: Start by clearly defining the change you are facing.
2. List Positive Outcomes: Write down at least three potential benefits or positive outcomes of this change.
3. Communicate: Share these positive aspects with relevant stakeholders—your team, peers, or family members.
4. Remind Yourself: Set calendar reminders to Periodically revisit and remind yourself of these benefits to maintain a positive perspective.
5. Reflect and Adjust: At the end of each day, reflect on your mindset toward change over the course of the day. How has focusing on the positives impacted your adaptability? Make any necessary adjustments to your mindset.

For Managers

As a manager, adopting this mindset can enhance your agility and help you lead your team through change with confidence. For example, a leader who is tasked with integrating AI into her team's operations is facing a lot of resistance and negativity from her team. She reflects back ten years ago when a different team she was leading had to replace their system of project management with a new software system. After persevering through that initial resistance, her new team went on to love the software. It even freed up time to do more meaningful work. Remembering this example can help her lead her team through this new change with a more positive mindset. She may even tell this story to her team to motivate them.

For Individual Contributors

For team members or individual contributors, looking on the bright side of change can improve productivity and well-being. When faced with changes in your project or work environment, take a moment to identify the positive outcomes that could arise. For instance, if your team is adopting a new software tool, instead of resisting the change, consider how it could enhance efficiency and make your tasks easier. Discuss these positives with your peers to collectively embrace the change. If a new process seems cumbersome at first, remind yourself and your colleagues of the long-term benefits.

For Home Life

At home, as a parent or spouse, applying this activity can help you enjoy the moment, manage your stress, and improve overall harmony. When family dynamics shift, such as moving to a new city or a child starting a new school, focus on the potential positives. Discuss these with your family to foster a supportive environment. For example, if you're relocating, instead of dwelling on the stress of moving, highlight the exciting opportunities for new experiences and friendships.

A positive outlook can help your family adapt more smoothly and cultivate a sense of adventure and satisfaction.

TAKE ACTION: This week, identify a recent change and list three positive outcomes to enhance your adaptability.

SM3. Focus on the Mission

When faced with challenges, the Stay Focused on the Mission Activity involves keeping your end goals in sight, regardless of obstacles. This exercise helps maintain clarity and resilience by continuously aligning actions with long-term objectives, even during turbulent times.

How to Do It:
1. Identify the Mission: Clearly define the overarching mission or end goal for your team, role, or family.
2. Communicate the Mission: Regularly share this mission with your team, peers, or family to ensure everyone is aligned.
3. Connect Daily Tasks: Relate daily activities and tasks to the broader mission to maintain focus and motivation.
4. Reflect Regularly: Take time to reflect on how current actions and decisions support the mission.
5. Reiterate During Challenges: When faced with obstacles, reiterate the mission to remind yourself and others of the long-term goals.

For Managers
As a manager, staying focused on the mission can be crucial when leading a team through significant changes, such as a merger or a restructuring. For example, during a corporate merger, employees might feel uncertain and anxious. Consistent communication about the overarching mission can help the team fight off being overwhelmed and stay focused on their day-to-day work. Regular check-ins and team meetings

to reiterate the mission can reinforce this focus and enhance resilience.

For Individual Contributors

For individual contributors, staying focused on the mission can be particularly helpful when dealing with day-to-day stressors and deadlines. Imagine facing a sudden project deadline that seems impossible to meet. By reminding yourself of the project's ultimate goal and its importance to the company's success, you can reframe the stress into a motivating factor. This focus can be maintained through quick, daily reflections on how your work aligns with the company's mission, boosting both resilience and performance in challenging situations.

For Home Life

At home, as a parent or spouse, staying focused on the mission can help in managing everyday family dynamics and unexpected challenges. For example, during a period of financial stress, the initial reaction might be anxiety and frustration. By focusing on the mission of maintaining a stable and nurturing environment for the family, you can approach the situation with a clearer mind and more constructive actions. Discussing family goals, such as prioritizing quality time together or supporting each other through tough times, can provide a grounding perspective. This approach not only strengthens resilience but also fosters a sense of unity and purpose within the family.

TAKE ACTION: This week, identify one long-term goal and reflect daily on how your actions support this mission.

SM4. Use a Decision-Making Matrix

The Decision-Making Matrix strategy involves systematically analyzing a situation to make informed choices rather than relying on gut instincts. Your gut can often be influenced by unconscious biases like recency bias or confirmation bias. This process encourages you to consider all relevant information, weigh the pros and cons, and predict potential outcomes before arriving at a decision.

How to Do It

1. Write Down Your Gut Decision: Don't think about it, just write down the decision you would make on an impulse.
2. Identify Your Choices: Clearly define possible choices you have.
3. List Out All Relevant Considerations: For example, if you're deciding on a car to buy you might include Style, Miles Per Gallon, and Safety.
4. Draw up a Matrix: Your decision choices run down the left-hand column, and your considerations are listed as their own columns to the right (see example).
5. Assign a Weight to Each Consideration on a Scale from 1-3: The idea is to rate how important each consideration is. For example, you might value the safety of a car at a three and the style at a one. Assign the weight right beneath the Consideration (see example).
6. Rate Each Choice by Consideration on a Scale from 1-3: Work your way through the matrix, assigning a number value.

7. Multiply Your Rating by its Weight: Multiply the weight by the consideration.

8. Calculate Your Final Score: Add up the total of each box. Now you have your "winner."

9. Compare Your Gut Decision to Your Ranked Decision: Is it different? The same? How might emotions have influenced your gut decision?

10. Review Your Decision: After implementing the matrix, review your decision and its outcomes to learn for future decisions.

For Managers

As a manager at work, employing a decision matrix can help you manage team conflicts more thoughtfully. Instead of reacting emotionally and potentially letting biases sway your decision, you can take a step back, gather all your options, and objectively evaluate the situation. For example, if two team members are clashing over project responsibilities, you can use a decision matrix together to list each person's suggestions, analyze how each option affects the team dynamics and project deadlines, and then decide on the best course of action. Running through the matrix together will help your team learn how to collaborate on a rational decision.

For Individual Contributors

As an individual contributor, the decision matrix can help you manage your workload. Consider a situation where you're unsure whether to take on an additional project. Instead of making an impulsive decision that could be influenced by recency bias, you can list the potential benefits, such as gaining new skills and recognition, against the drawbacks, like increased stress and potential burnout. By weighing these factors and evaluating their importance, you can make a more informed choice that aligns with your long-term goals and capacity.

For Home Life

At home, as a parent or spouse, the decision-making matrix can be a valuable tool for resolving family conflicts. For instance, if there's a disagreement about whether to move to a new city for a job opportunity, this method can help. Your family can list the pros and cons of the move, such as career advancement and better schools versus the challenges, such as leaving friends and adapting to a new environment. By considering everyone's perspective and listing out all of your options, your family can arrive at a decision that feels balanced and fair.

Example Decision Matrix

Car Options	Style (Weight=1)	Miles per gallon (2)	Safety (3)	Cost (3)	Final Score
Option 1:					
Option 2:					
Option 3:					

Example Decision Matrix: Scored and Weighted

Car Options	Style (1)	Miles per gallon (2)	Safety (3)	Cost (3)	Final Score
Option 1:	3	1	1	1	

Car Options	Style (1)	Miles per gallon (2)	Safety (3)	Cost (3)	Final Score
Option 2:	1	3	3	3	
Option 3:	3	2	2	1	

Example Decision Matrix: Score Times Weight, and Total Score

Car Options	Style (1)	Miles per gallon (2)	Safety (3)	Cost (3)	Final Score
Option 1:	3 X 1 = 3	1 X 2= 2	1 X 3 = 3	1 X 3 = 3	11
Option 2:	1 X 1 = 1	3 X 2 = 6	3 X 3 = 9	3 X 3 = 9	25
Option 3:	3 X 1 = 3	2 X 2 = 4	2 X 3 = 6	1 X 3 = 3	20

TAKE ACTION: This week, create a decision matrix for a challenging decision to see how it improves your outcome.

SM5. Reframe Negative Situations

The Positive Reframing Activity is a powerful technique where you reinterpret negative or challenging situations in a positive way. This activity can transform your approach to life by helping you see positive possibilities when bad things happen.

How to Do It:

1. Identify the Situation: Recognize a challenging or negative situation you are currently facing.
2. Pause and Reflect: Take a moment to step back and distance yourself emotionally from the immediate reaction.
3. List Negative Thoughts: Write down your initial negative thoughts and feelings about the situation.
4. Find Positive Aspects: Actively look for and list positive aspects or potential benefits within the situation.
5. Reframe Your Perspective: Consciously reinterpret the situation by focusing on the positive aspects and potential growth opportunities.
6. Plan Your Response: Decide on a constructive and balanced response based on your reframed perspective.

For Managers

As a manager at work, you often face high-pressure situations that demand swift and effective responses. Implementing the Positive Reframing Activity can help you navigate these moments with greater clarity. For instance, when faced with an underperforming team member, instead of immediately reacting with frustration, you can reframe the situation by seeing it as an opportunity for you to develop your patience and coaching skills.

For Individual Contributors

In any career there will be times of frustration. Imagine being passed over for a promotion that you felt you deserved. While of course you should allow yourself to feel disappointed (it's natural), you could also reframe this moment as an opportunity to grow. You can use this time to develop new skills or take on extra responsibilities within your role. By strengthening your qualifications, you'll increase your odds for the next promotion.

For Home Life

At home, as a parent or spouse, the Positive Reframing Activity can help you see your daily tasks in a new light. For example, if you are feeling frustrated or bored with driving your kids to school every day or to all their weekend activities, you might reframe it by remembering that you have very few weekends until they head off to college. These simple drives might lead to snippets of meaningful conversation, and you might look back at them fondly.

TAKE ACTION: This week, choose one challenging situation and reinterpret it in a positive way to find a more productive perspective.

SM6. Replace Unhelpful Thoughts with Cognitive Restructuring

Cognitive restructuring is a strategy used in cognitive behavioral therapy (CBT). You can just as easily use it in your daily life. Cognitive restructuring is about identifying and challenging unhelpful thoughts and replacing them with more balanced, realistic ones. This is a powerful way to manage your emotions and reactions.

How to Do It

1. Identify the Thought: Recognize the specific thought that is causing you distress or negative emotions.
2. Examine the Evidence: Assess the evidence for and against this thought. Consider all perspectives.
3. Challenge the Thought: Ask yourself if the thought is rational, based on facts, or driven by emotions.
4. Reframe the Thought: Develop a more balanced, constructive thought that is realistic and positive.
5. Practice Regularly: Incorporate this technique into your daily routine, such as during a quiet moment or when reflecting on the day.

For Managers

As a manager, your team looks to you and your attitude for inspiration. Cognitive restructuring can help you stay confident and positive. For instance, if a project is behind schedule and you feel overwhelmed, you might find yourself thinking, "I'm failing as a leader." By restructuring this thought, you can consider more constructive alternatives like, "This is a challenging situation, but I have the skills to navigate it and lead my team to success."

For Individual Contributors

As a team member, cognitive restructuring can help you fight off insecurity and defensiveness when you receive feedback. Suppose a colleague criticizes your work, and your initial reaction is, "They don't value my contributions." Instead, you might reframe this thought as "They are trying to help me. They may have useful feedback that can help me improve. I should at least consider it carefully."

For Home Life

At home, as a parent or spouse, cognitive restructuring can help you stop yourself from negative ruminations and blaming. If you find yourself feeling frustrated with a partner or child and think, "They *never* listen to me," try reframing it to, "*Often* they don't listen to me when they're stressed out. I'll recommunicate my needs and boundaries at a different time when they are unhurried and I have their full attention."

TAKE ACTION: This week, identify one negative thought each day and reframe it using cognitive restructuring to improve your self-management skills.

SM7. Control Impulses with Stop-Think-Act

The Stop-Think-Act strategy is a simple yet powerful method for managing your reactions in challenging situations. To navigate stressful moments with greater clarity and control, simply 1) pause to assess the situation, 2) think about the best course of action, and 3) act accordingly.

How to Do It

1. Stop: Pause before reacting to any challenging situation. Take a deep breath and give yourself a moment to gather your thoughts.
2. Think: Consider the situation objectively. Reflect on the best course of action, taking into account all perspectives and potential outcomes.
3. Act: Respond thoughtfully and constructively. Implement the action you have decided on and communicate clearly with others involved.
4. Practice Regularly: Incorporate the Stop-Think-Act trick into your daily routine. Use it during meetings, collaborations, and family interactions to make it a habit.

For Managers

As a manager, you have to stay collected and composed even in high-pressure moments. Using the Stop-Think-Act trick can help you slow down and avoid letting your emotions hijack your actions. For example, if a team member misses an important deadline and your initial reaction is to reprimand them:

1. Take a moment to stop.
2. Think about the possible reasons behind the delay and the best way to address the issue constructively.
3. Then, act by discussing the situation with the team member to understand their perspective and find a solution.

For Individual Contributors

For an individual contributor, Stop-Think-Act can help you avoid snap judgments and reactions and help you receive feedback more graciously. Suppose a colleague criticizes your work in a meeting, and your instinct is to react defensively. Instead, you might 1) stop and take a deep breath, 2) think about their feedback objectively and consider how it might help improve your work, and 3) act by responding calmly and expressing your willingness to discuss their concerns further. Practice this approach during peer reviews and collaborative projects when emotions tend to run high.

For Home Life

At home, as a parent or spouse, the Stop-Think-Act trick can save you from saying or doing something you'll regret. When faced with a frustrating situation, such as a child refusing to do their homework or a partner forgetting an important date, your first impulse might be to react emotionally. Instead, 1) stop and take a moment to collect your thoughts, 2) think about the underlying issues and the most effective way to address them, and 3) act by communicating your feelings calmly and working together to find a solution.

TAKE ACTION: This week, practice the Stop-Think-Act trick at least once a day to enhance your self-management skills and improve your reactions in challenging situations.

SM8. Use Box Breathing to Manage Stress

Box breathing, also known as four-square breathing, is a simple yet powerful technique used to manage stress and enhance focus. It involves inhaling for four seconds, holding your breath four seconds, exhaling for four seconds, and holding again for four seconds. This practice helps to calm the mind, reduce anxiety, and improve concentration.

How to Do It

1. Sit Comfortably: Keep your back straight and your feet flat on the floor.
2. Close your Eyes, Inhale Deeply through your Nose for a Count of Four.
3. Hold Your Breath for a Count of Four.
4. Exhale Slowly and Completely through Your Mouth for a Count of Four.
5. Hold Your Breath again for a Count of Four.
6. Repeat the Cycle at Least Four Times: Or wait until you feel more centered and calm.

For Managers

As a manager, dealing with a high-pressure environment can often lead to stress and emotional overwhelm. Integrating box breathing can alleviate stress in just a couple of minutes. For instance, before a critical meeting or after a challenging interaction with a team member, take a few minutes to practice box breathing. This can help reset your mind and approach the situation with clarity and composure. Imagine dealing with a team conflict where emotions are high.

A few minutes of box breathing can help you remain calm and respond thoughtfully rather than react impulsively or in a state of panic.

For Individual Contributors

For team members, navigating the dynamics of workplace relationships can be equally stressful. Whether you're preparing for a presentation or dealing with feedback, practicing box breathing can center your thoughts and reduce anxiety. Suppose you're about to deliver an important presentation to your colleagues. Just before stepping into the room, find a quiet space and engage in a few cycles of box breathing. This can help calm your nerves, allowing you to present with greater confidence and clarity. By approaching the presentation with a centered mind, you're more likely to communicate effectively and make a positive impression.

For Home Life

At home, whether you're a parent or a spouse, transitioning from work to home can be mentally tough. Box breathing can help you clear your mind, reduce work anxiety, and enter your home feeling refreshed and ready to be a good spouse and parent.

TAKE ACTION: This week, incorporate box breathing before a stressful event and notice the difference in your emotional response.

SM9. Take a Systematic Approach to Problem Solving

Take a systematic approach to problem solving to manage your stress and avoid impulsive decisions. By applying each of the steps below when you next face a problem, you can manage stress and react more thoughtfully.

How to Do It

1. Identify the Problem: Clearly define the issue you're facing. Be specific about what the problem is and why it's a problem.
2. Gather Information: Collect all relevant data and perspectives to fully understand the problem.
3. Generate Possible Solutions: Brainstorm a list of potential solutions with input from multiple people. Don't evaluate them yet; just focus on generating as many ideas as possible.
4. Evaluate Solutions: Weigh all options by assessing the feasibility, advantages, and disadvantages of each solution. Consider the potential impact and resources required.
5. Choose the Best Solution: Select the solution that appears to be the most effective and practical.
6. Implement the Solution: Put the chosen solution into action. Ensure you have a plan in place for its execution.
7. Review the Outcome: After implementation, review the results. Determine whether the problem has been resolved and what you can learn from the process.

For Managers

As a manager, you're often faced with complex challenges that require quick yet effective decisions. A problem-solving strategy can help you navigate these situations with greater ease. For example, if you're leading a marketing team that's experiencing a sudden drop in LinkedIn Ad performance, you might be tempted to push your team to work long hours to create new ads. However, it will likely serve you better to take a step back to gather information and analyze the situation. Involve your team in brainstorming potential solutions and weigh all the options by evaluating their pros and cons. You might find a small tweak in your messaging or landing page solves the whole problem. As a leader, this more structured approach to problem solving not only helps you find the best solution, but it also fosters a collaborative environment where team members feel valued and heard.

For Individual Contributors

For team members, workplace dynamics can sometimes lead to conflicts or misunderstandings. Implementing problem-solving strategies can help you address these issues constructively. Imagine you're working on a project and you disagree with a colleague about the best approach. Instead of reacting defensively or aggressively, use problem-solving steps: Gather information to identify the root cause of your disagreement, brainstorm multiple solutions together, and weigh all options based on their feasibility and impact. This method not only helps resolve the conflict, but it also strengthens your professional relationship.

For Home Life

At home, whether you're a parent or a spouse, daily life can bring about any number of challenges that test your patience and composure. For instance, if your child is struggling with their homework, instead of reacting with impatience, guide them through a problem-solving process. Help them gather information to understand the problem, brainstorm solutions, and weigh all options to evaluate which one might work best. This not only assists in resolving the immediate issue but also teaches them this valuable problem-solving framework they can use in the future.

TAKE ACTION: This week, use a structured problem-solving approach to tackle a challenging situation and observe the impact on your reactivity and self-management.

SM10. Interrupt Negative Thoughts with "Thought Stopping"

Thought stopping is a technique that helps interrupt and redirect intrusive or negative thoughts. By recognizing when these thoughts occur and actively stopping them, you can improve focus and emotional control.

How to Do It

1. Recognize the Thought: Be aware of when an intrusive or negative thought occurs. Awareness is the first step in managing these thoughts.
2. Interrupt the Thought: Use a specific cue or command like "Stop!" to interrupt your negative thought. You can do this mentally or verbally.
3. Replace the Thought: Immediately replace your negative thought with a more positive or neutral one. This shift helps redirect your focus and emotional state.
4. Practice Regularly: Consistency is key. Practice thought stopping regularly to make it a habit and increase its effectiveness.
5. Review and Reflect: After using thought stopping, take a moment to reflect on its impact. Consider how it changed your emotional response and what you can learn from the experience.

For Managers

As a manager, navigating the complexities of leading a team can sometimes lead to stress and negative thought patterns. Thought stopping can be a valuable tool in these situations. For example, if you find yourself thinking, "I can't handle this workload," or "I'm never going to hit this deadline," interrupt that thought with a firm "Stop!" and replace it with, "I can break this down into manageable steps."

For Individual Contributors

For team members, workplace interactions and pressures can often trigger negative thoughts, impacting performance and relationships. Imposter syndrome, where you doubt your abilities and fear being exposed as a fraud, is a common issue. Imagine you're about to present your work to the team or to meet a big client to pitch a new project, and the thought, "I'm not good enough to be here," keeps circling through your head. Use thought stopping to halt this negative thought. Then, replace that thought with something constructive. For example, you might think, "I have earned my place here and my work is valuable." This approach can reduce anxiety, improve confidence, and enhance your overall work experience.

For Home Life

At home, whether you're a parent or a spouse, daily stresses can lead to recurring negative thoughts. For instance, if your child is having a tantrum and you're thinking, "I'm a terrible parent," you can use thought stopping to break your negative cycle. Replace that thought with, "I'm doing my best, and this is just a challenging moment." Similarly, during a disagreement with your spouse, if a thought like, "They never understand me," comes up, you can interrupt it and reframe it to something more productive and forward-moving, like, "We can work through this together."

TAKE ACTION: This week, practice thought stopping whenever a negative thought arises.

SM11. Pre-commit to Bind Yourself to Important Actions

Pre-commitment strategies involve making a decision in advance to bind yourself to a desired course of action. This technique helps ensure that you follow through on your intentions, especially when faced with temptations or distractions that might derail you. A classic example of this is in sales where you're directed to "close" at the end of a conversation. By planning to "close" before the call even begins, you ensure that you try.

How to Do It

1. Identify Your Goal: Clearly define the objective you want to achieve. Be specific about what you intend to accomplish.

2. Create a Plan: Outline the steps you need to take to reach your goal. Include specific actions and deadlines.

3. Make It Public: Share your commitment with others to create accountability. This could be with your team, colleagues, or family members.

4. Set Up Reminders: Use tools like calendars, alarms, or apps to remind you of your commitments and deadlines.

5. Monitor Progress: Regularly check your progress towards your goal. Adjust your plan as necessary to stay on track.

6. Reflect and Adjust: After completing your commitment, reflect on what worked and what didn't. Use these insights to improve future pre-commitments.

For Managers

As a manager, you can use pre-commitment strategies to pro-actively invest your time into proper priorities. For example, if you tend to react to the crises of the day and work "in the weeds," you might find yourself looking at the clock frustrated at the end of the day as you keep pushing back your bigger-picture strategic thinking. To disrupt this pattern, pre-commit time for strategic thinking by scheduling dedicated time blocks in your calendar and protecting that time. If your introverted nature keeps you focused on solo tasks while neglecting relationship building, you can pre-commit to stopping by team members' offices and attending networking events. By making these commitments public, you create accountability. This helps you stay on track and sets a positive example for your team about the importance of planning and time management.

For Individual Contributors

For team members, pre-commitment can be a powerful tool to improve productivity. Suppose you're working on a project with tight deadlines and you have a tendency to get sidetracked by less critical tasks. You can pre-commit by creating a detailed task list, setting specific deadlines for each task, and sharing this plan with your colleagues. You could also pre-commit to due dates every time your manager asks you to do something. By clarifying deadlines and creating detailed task lists in advance, you reduce the likelihood of procrastination.

For Home Life

At home, whether you're a parent or a spouse, pre-commitment strategies can help you strike a better work-life balance. For instance, if you find it challenging to spend quality time with your family due to a busy schedule, you can pre-commit by designating certain evenings or weekends as family time. Communicate this to your family members so they can hold you accountable. This will also strengthen your relationships by showing your family that you value and respect your time with them.

TAKE ACTION: This week, pre-commit to a specific goal and share your plan with someone to increase your accountability and follow-through.

SM12. Define and Set Clear Boundaries

Setting boundaries is a crucial activity to manage your time, energy, and emotional well-being. By clearly defining what you will and will not accept in various aspects of your life, you can maintain focus, reduce stress, and improve overall productivity.

How to Do It

1. Identify Your Priorities: Determine what is most important to you in different areas of your life.
2. Define Clear Boundaries: Specify what you will and will not accept. Be precise about your limits.
3. Communicate Boundaries: Clearly communicate your boundaries to relevant parties, explaining the reasons behind them.
4. Set Up Reminders: Use tools like calendars, alarms, or apps to remind yourself and others of your boundaries.
5. Be Consistent: Stick to your boundaries consistently to reinforce their importance.
6. Adjust as Needed: Boundaries can and should change with your needs. Regularly review your boundaries and make adjustments based on feedback and changing circumstances.
7. Reflect and Learn: After implementing boundaries, reflect on their effectiveness and make improvements as necessary.

For Managers

As a manager, setting boundaries is vital for maintaining a productive work environment. For instance, you might establish "no meeting" times during certain hours of the day to focus on strategic planning or high-priority tasks. Communicate these boundaries clearly to your team, explaining the importance of uninterrupted time for critical work. This also sets a positive example for your team, and it makes it so that you don't feel guilty for "going quiet" during your uninterrupted hours. Suppose you receive constant interruptions from team members needing immediate feedback. By setting a boundary, such as designated office hours, you can ensure that your essential work time is protected while still making yourself available to your team.

For Individual Contributors

For team members, workplace boundaries can help you focus on your most important tasks and ensure that your boss or teammates don't take too much from you emotionally. For example, if you find that you're frequently staying late because of last-minute requests, it's important to set boundaries to protect your personal time. Communicate with your peers about your availability and the best times to reach you for non-urgent matters. For example, you could set a boundary by informing your colleagues that you will be checking emails in batches at specific times during the day. This allows you to focus on your tasks without constant disruption.

For Home Life

At home, boundaries are equally important for fostering healthy relationships and managing responsibilities. As a parent or spouse who works from home, you may struggle with balancing work and family time. Setting clear boundaries can help you be more present and engaged with your loved ones. For instance, you could establish a rule that family dinners are a device-free time, allowing for meaningful conversations without the distraction of phones or work emails. Similarly, setting boundaries around work hours—such as not checking work emails after 7 PM—can help you unwind and focus on family interactions. This strengthens family relationships and helps you recharge.

TAKE ACTION: This week, identify one area where you need better boundaries, set a clear limit, and communicate it to those affected.

SM13. Practice Gratitude

Practicing gratitude involves consciously focusing on the positive aspects of your life and feeling a deep sense of appreciation for them. This simple yet powerful activity can shift your mindset and enhance your well-being.

How to Do It

1. Set Aside Time Daily: Dedicate a few minutes each day to reflect on what you are grateful for. This can be done in the morning or before bed.

2. Be Specific: When thinking about gratitude, be specific about what you are thankful for and why it matters to you.

3. Internal Reflection: Take a moment to internalize your feelings of gratitude. Feel the positive emotions associated with what you appreciate.

4. Keep a Gratitude Journal: Write down three things you are grateful for each day to reinforce positive thinking and mindfulness.

5. Start Meetings with Gratitude: Begin team meetings with a moment of personal reflection on what everyone is grateful for to set a positive tone.

6. Encourage a Gratitude Culture: Foster a culture of gratitude by encouraging team members and families to reflect on their own feelings of thankfulness.

7. Reflect on the Impact: Regularly reflect on how feeling and practicing gratitude has affected your mindset and relationships.

For Managers

As a manager, fostering a sense of gratitude can help you quash your negative emotions, appreciate the people around you, and create an atmosphere of positivity. You might set aside time to regularly reflect on the positive contributions of your team and the progress you've made together. Former Campbell's Soup CEO, Doug Conant, used to handwrite 20 thank you notes a day to employees. He once explained that this gratitude practice didn't just boost company morale, but it guaranteed he'd go home with a positive mindset at the end of each day.

For Individual Contributors

As a team member, cultivating gratitude can help you feel less overwhelmed, less stressed out, and more appreciative of what you already have. For example, if you find yourself frustrated by the fact that you haven't yet been promoted, take some time to reflect on what you're grateful for now—your work-life balance, the growth opportunities you've had, and your team members who have become your friends. This reflection might help you feel more satisfied with where you're at and patient about your future. In turn, this can help you to continue to work toward that promotion without losing motivation.

For Home Life

At home, daily life can be filled with responsibilities. Taking time to appreciate the small moments and positive aspects of your family life can make a big difference. For instance, reflecting on your gratitude for your partner's support after a long day can help you show your appreciation and make your spouse feel seen. Similarly, taking the time to appreciate the way your kid gets so passionate about soccer can make driving them home from practice after a long day of work feel more enjoyable and less like a chore.

TAKE ACTION: This week, take a few minutes each day to reflect on what you're grateful for and observe the impact on your mood and relationships.

SOCIAL AWARENESS STRATEGIES

Social awareness involves recognizing and understanding the emotions, needs, and concerns of others, allowing you to navigate social complexities with empathy and insight. This ability enhances your interactions, fosters meaningful connections, and helps you build strong, supportive relationships.

In this chapter, you will discover a variety of strategies to perceive social cues accurately, increase your ability to see others' perspectives, and deepen your empathy.

1. **Practice Active Listening:** Engage in active listening to fully comprehend what others are saying and understand the emotions behind their words.

2. **Grow Your Body Language Awareness:** Tune into non-verbal cues such as facial expressions, tone of voice, and posture to gather information about the emotional state of others.

3. **Ask Open-Ended Questions:** Encourage deeper conversations by asking open-ended questions that require more than a yes or no response like, "And what else?" or "Tell me more."

4. **Master "Time and Place" Awareness:** Recognize the appropriateness of discussing certain topics depending on the social context.

5. **Understand Boundaries:** Be aware of personal boundaries and respect others' comfort zones.

6. **Learn Your Group's Dynamics:** Understand the politics and emotional undercurrents within a group setting. Consider things like titles, who sits where, who is deferential to whom, and who interrupts others.

7. **Observe Facial Expressions in Movies:** Spend time watching movies, shows, or videos with the sound off, and try to infer the emotional states of the characters solely through their facial expressions.

8. **Grow Your Cultural Sensitivity :** Seek to educate yourself about different cultural norms. Ask your colleagues about their traditions.

9. **Practice Perspective-Taking:** Make a conscious effort to see things from another person's viewpoint.

10. **Note Introverted and Extroverted Traits:** Observe how your colleagues interact. Notice behaviors like who tends to speak up and who remains quiet, and consider how these behaviors might relate to their introverted or extroverted tendencies.

11. **Observe and Understand People's Goals and Motivations:** Take a moment to observe and understand what motivates the people around you.

12. **Ask Power Questions:** Instead of closed or simple questions, use powerful open-ended questions. This will invite meaningful conversations and provide insights into the other person's motivations, experiences, and interests.

13. **Scan the Energy of the Room:** Each time you enter a room, take a moment to observe the atmosphere and the interactions taking place. Notice the energy levels,

who is engaging with whom, and the overall mood of the group.

SoA1. Practice Active Listening

Active listening involves fully concentrating, understanding, responding, and remembering what the other person is saying. Active listening skills enable you to foster deeper connections, understand the people around you more deeply, and create an empathetic environment.

How to Do It

1. Give Full Attention: Focus completely on the speaker without distractions. Maintain eye contact and be present in the moment.
2. Acknowledge the Speaker: Use nods, smiles, and short verbal affirmations like "I see" or "I understand" to show you are engaged.
3. Reflect and Paraphrase: Summarize what the speaker has said in your own words to check your understanding. For example, "So what you're saying is..."
4. Ask Open-Ended Questions: Encourage further discussion by asking questions that require more than yes or no answers.
5. Avoid Interrupting: Let the speaker finish their thoughts without cutting in or redirecting the conversation.
6. Provide Feedback: Share your thoughts and responses after the speaker has finished, showing that you have thoughtfully considered their words.
7. Practice Regularly: Make active listening a habit in all your interactions to continually improve your communication skills.

For Managers

As a manager, practicing active listening can help create an open and psychologically safe environment. For example, during one-on-one meetings with your team members, focus entirely on the speaker without interrupting or formulating your response while they speak. This shows respect and genuine interest in their concerns and ideas. It also ensures that you are tuned into what they're saying and how they're feeling. Suppose a team member expresses frustration about a project. By actively listening and asking follow-up questions like, "Can you tell me more about what's challenging?" you demonstrate empathy, and you can learn more about their challenge which enables you to address it. Active listening empowers your team to share openly, and it models the way everyone should treat the person on your team who is speaking.

For Individual Contributors

For team members, active listening helps ensure that everyone feels heard and valued, reducing misunderstandings and fostering a more cooperative team dynamic. For example, when working on a group project, make an effort to listen to your peers' contributions without immediately jumping in with your thoughts. If a colleague is explaining their perspective on a task, acknowledge their viewpoint by paraphrasing and asking clarifying questions such as, "So you're saying you think we should approach it this way because...?"

For Home Life

At home, it can be all too easy to treat what your spouse or kids say as a part of your routine. Taking the time to listen closely, without distraction, can deepen your relationships with family members. For instance, when your child talks about their day, put aside your phone and give them your full attention. Reflect on their feelings by saying, "It sounds like you had a really exciting day at school. What was your favorite part?" This shows that you care and encourages them to open up more. You'll also learn a lot more about what matters to your kid and how they're really feeling.

TAKE ACTION: This week, practice active listening in all your conversations to enhance your social awareness and build deeper connections.

SoA2. Grow Your Body Language Awareness

Reading body language involves observing and interpreting non-verbal cues such as facial expressions, gestures, posture, and eye movements. By honing this skill, you can gain insights into others' emotions and intentions, leading to more effective and empathetic interactions.

How to Do It

1. Observe Carefully: Pay close attention to people's facial expressions, gestures, posture, and eye movements during interactions.

2. Look for Patterns: Identify consistent non-verbal cues that might indicate specific emotions or states of mind.

3. Context Matters: Consider the context in which the body language occurs. The same gesture can mean different things in different situations.

4. Mirror and Validate: Reflect back what you observe verbally to validate your interpretation. For example, "You seem a bit uncomfortable. Is everything okay?"

5. Practice Empathy: Put yourself in the other person's shoes to understand their feelings and perspectives better.

6. Seek Feedback: Ask for feedback on your interpretations to improve your understanding and accuracy over time.

7. Continue Learning: Stay informed about the nuances of body language through books, courses, and real-life practice.

For Managers

As a manager, being adept at reading body language can help you to be more proactive in your empathy and your care for your team members. For instance, during team meetings, you might notice a team member crossing their arms and avoiding eye contact. This could indicate discomfort or disagreement. Noticing this non-verbal cue, you can then address it by asking for their input.

For Individual Contributors

For team members, paying attention to body language can help you treat your coworkers with more care. Imagine you're collaborating on your team's quarterly report, and you notice your colleague frequently looking away and fidgeting during discussions. These signals might suggest they are feeling overwhelmed or unsure. You might check in with them to see how they're feeling about the project. They may just need a bit more clarification, or you might find that they're distracted by something completely outside the realm of your project. Without noticing those early signals, you might have just chalked it up to them being lazy or disinterested.

For Home Life

At home, reading body language can give you insights into how your family members are feeling. In turn, this can open up important conversations. For example, if your child comes home from school and avoids eye contact while responding curtly, it could signify they had a tough day. You might offer comfort or open up a dialogue to learn more about their day and give them a chance to vent.

TAKE ACTION: This week, observe the body language of people in your meetings, your boss at different times of the day, and your spouse when they seem stressed. Use these observations to enhance your social awareness.

SoA3. Ask Open-Ended Questions

Asking open-ended questions involves prompting others to share more detailed and expansive responses. These questions, which typically begin with "how," "why," or "what," encourage people to express their thoughts, feelings, and experiences more fully. Open-ended questions are a great way to foster deeper conversations and understanding.

How to Do It

1. Start with 'What,' 'How,' or 'Why:' Frame your questions to encourage detailed responses rather than simple yes or no answers.
2. Be Curious: Show genuine interest in the other person's thoughts and feelings.
3. Listen Actively: Pay close attention to the responses, showing that you value what they are saying.
4. Avoid Interrupting: Let the other person finish their thoughts before responding or asking another question.
5. Follow Up: Ask additional open-ended questions based on their responses to deepen the conversation.
6. Be Patient: Give the other person time to think and respond thoughtfully.
7. Practice Regularly: Make a habit of using open-ended questions in your daily interactions to improve your skills over time.

For Managers

As a manager, asking open-ended questions can help you gather valuable feedback and create an environment where team members feel heard and appreciated. For instance, during team meetings, instead of asking, "Do you understand the task?" you might ask, "How are you thinking about this objective?" You might even invite others to participate in problem solving. You could ask, "That is one way to proceed, but what are some other ideas? What do you think we're missing?" This approach invites team members to share their perspectives and insights, revealing any potential concerns or suggestions they might have.

For Individual Contributors

For team members, employing open-ended questions demonstrates genuine interest, and prompts the other person to reflect more deeply and share more comprehensively . When someone shares an idea or perspective, follow up with "And what else?" or "tell me more." This invites them to delve further into their thoughts, revealing additional layers of information that might not surface otherwise.

For Home Life

At home, asking open-ended questions can help you move past smaller, surface-level conversations to something deeper and more meaningful. As a parent or spouse, rather than asking, "Did you have a good day?" you could ask, "What was the most interesting part of your day?" This invites your family members to open up about their experiences and feelings, promoting deeper connections and understanding. For example, if your child seems upset after school, an open-ended question can provide them with an opportunity to share their concerns. And the open-ended question will help you do so without coming across as nosy or invasive.

TAKE ACTION: This week, focus on asking open-ended questions in your conversations to unlock deeper understanding and empathy in your interactions.

SoA4. Master "Time and Place" Awareness

Time and place awareness is about understanding and being mindful of the context of your interactions. This means you consider the appropriateness of timing and setting. The classic example of someone who is bad at time and place awareness is the coworker who brags about how hard they partied the night before, not considering what this might imply about their preparedness and professionalism.

How to Do It

1. Assess the Context: Consider the current situation and emotional state of those involved before initiating a conversation.

2. Choose the Right Setting: Select a location that is private and comfortable for discussing sensitive topics.

3. Pick an Appropriate Time: Avoid times of high stress or distraction. Aim for moments when everyone is more likely to be calm and receptive.

4. Prepare in Advance: Think about what you want to say and how you want to say it, ensuring it's suitable for the context.

5. Observe Reactions: Pay attention to the body language and responses of others to gauge if the timing and setting are appropriate.

6. Adjust if Necessary: If you sense discomfort or distraction, be ready to suggest rescheduling the conversation.

7. Reflect and Learn: After the conversation, reflect on

what went well and what could be improved for future interactions.

For Managers

As a manager, understanding when and where to address certain topics with your team signals respect for their feelings and can lead to more productive and positive conversations. For instance, delivering constructive feedback requires a private, comfortable setting where your team member can feel at ease and open to discussion. Choosing the right time is equally important; it's best to avoid moments of high stress or tight deadlines. Suppose you need to discuss performance improvements with a team member. Instead of addressing this issue in the middle of an already hectic meeting, schedule a private, dedicated time in your office.

For Individual Contributors

For team members, being aware of the appropriate time and place to bring up ideas or concerns can make your colleagues more receptive to and prepared for a constructive discussion. Imagine you have an innovative idea for a project but choose to bring it up during a busy period when everyone is focused on urgent tasks. The idea might not get the attention it deserves. Instead, consider presenting your idea during a team brainstorming session or during open-ended time in one-on-one with your manager.

For Home Life

At home, understanding the right moments to have serious discussions is crucial. For example, if you need to discuss a sensitive topic with your partner, it's better to wait until you're both relaxed and free from distractions rather than bringing it up right after a long day at work. Similarly, with children, choosing a calm time, such as during a family meal or a quiet evening, can make them more open to talking about their feelings and experiences. This approach fosters a supportive and understanding family environment.

TAKE ACTION: This week, practice time and place awareness by choosing appropriate moments for important conversations to enhance your social interactions.

SoA5. Understand Boundaries

Respecting people's boundaries at work is key to a healthy and productive work environment. It's about understanding what makes your colleagues comfortable and maintaining a professional distance that allows everyone to focus on their tasks. Boundaries may include availability, work style, or personal space.

How to Do It:

1. Observe and Listen: Pay attention to verbal and non-verbal cues that indicate someone's boundaries.
2. Ask Directly: When in doubt, ask about boundaries respectfully. For example, you might ask, "Is it okay if we discuss this now?"
3. Acknowledge Boundaries: Verbally acknowledge and respect the boundaries set by others.
4. Communicate Clearly: If you need to ask for a favor that might infringe on someone's boundary, communicate your respect for their limit first.
5. Model Respect: Demonstrate your own boundaries and respect others' boundaries to set a standard.
6. Follow Up: Check back with the person to ensure their boundaries were respected and any potential issues were addressed.

For Managers

As a manager, respecting your team members' boundaries preserves their trust and promotes a healthy work-life balance. For instance, if a team member has made it clear that they prefer not to work weekends or weekday evenings, refrain from sending work-related messages during that time. If an urgent situation arises, communicate your understanding of their boundary before requesting their assistance. For example, saying, "I know you usually don't work on weekends, but we have a critical issue. Could you help with this?"

For Individual Contributors

For an individual contributor, being mindful of your peers' boundaries can help foster a cooperative and supportive work environment. Suppose a colleague has a closed office door, signaling their need for uninterrupted work time. Instead of barging in with a question, consider sending a quick message asking if you can discuss something when they are free. This simple act of respect can prevent unnecessary disruptions and show that you value their concentration and productivity.

For Home Life

At home, respecting boundaries is equally important in maintaining healthy relationships. Imagine your spouse has had a long day and prefers not to discuss certain stressful topics, like finances. Acknowledging their need for a peaceful evening by saying, "I know you've had a tough day, let's talk about this another time," can help them feel supported and understood. Similarly, with children, respecting their boundaries, such as not entering their room without permission, can promote trust and respect within the family.

TAKE ACTION: This week, make a conscious effort to observe and respect the boundaries of at least one person in your daily interactions.

SoA6. Learn Your Group's Dynamics

Observe your group's interactions during your next team meeting or family discussion. Notice who speaks first, who listens, and who seems to influence decisions. This exercise isn't about taking notes or analyzing data. Instead, it's about tuning into the social currents that define your work and home environments.

How to Do It

1. Observe Without Intervening: During meetings or family discussions, focus on observing rather than participating.
2. Note Patterns: Look for recurring behaviors, such as who initiates conversations, who gets interrupted, and who supports others' ideas.
3. Identify Key Influencers: Recognize individuals who seem to hold sway over group opinions, regardless of their formal role or title.
4. Reflect on Your Role: Consider how your actions might influence group dynamics and what changes you can make to foster a more positive environment.
5. Act on Insights: Use your observations to adjust your approach, whether it's amplifying quieter voices, leveraging influencers, or creating a more inclusive atmosphere.

For Managers

As a manager, understanding the subtleties of your group dynamics enables you to better navigate team emotions and resolve conflicts. For example, during a brainstorming session, you might notice that while everyone turns to a particular team member for validation, this person doesn't hold a senior title. Recognizing this, you can leverage that person's influence to drive engagement.

For Individual Contributors

For an individual contributor, awareness of your team's dynamics can help you adjust your communication style. This makes it easier to collaborate and build stronger working relationships. Suppose you're part of a project team and you see a colleague consistently yielding to another's opinion, even if they have valid points. By observing this dynamic, you can identify opportunities to support your quieter peers, fostering a more balanced exchange of ideas.

For Home Life

At home, awareness of family dynamics can help you manage family emotions and create opportunities for every family member to express themselves. During family discussions, take note of who usually takes the lead, who remains silent, and whose opinions are quickly dismissed. For instance, you might find that one child often feels overlooked. Knowing this, you can be sure to give them opportunities to have the floor and express themselves.

TAKE ACTION: This week, observe the group dynamics in your next meeting and note who influences decisions the most.

SoA7. Observe Facial Expressions in the Movies

Next time you watch a movie, try turning off the sound and focus solely on the actors' facial expressions and body language. This activity helps you hone your ability to read non-verbal cues and understand emotions without relying on dialogue.

How to Do It
1. Choose a Movie: Select a movie with strong character-driven stories and expressive actors.
2. Turn Off the Sound: Watch the movie without any sound to focus solely on visual cues.
3. Observe Facial Expressions: Pay close attention to the actors' facial expressions during different scenes.
4. Note Body Language: Observe how body language complements or contrasts with facial expressions.
5. Reflect on Emotions: Try to interpret the emotions being conveyed without dialogue.
6. Apply Insights: Use your observations to better understand and respond to non-verbal cues in real-life interactions.

For Managers
As a manager, the ability to read facial expressions and body language can enable you to tune into the needs of your team members more closely. For example, during a team meeting, you might notice a team member who seems disengaged based on the fact that they're slumped in their chair and keep looking away and yawning. By recognizing these cues,

you can address their concerns proactively. You might pull them aside after the meeting to check in and offer support.

For Individual Contributors

For an individual contributor, understanding non-verbal cues can help you become more attuned to the unspoken messages your teammates convey. Suppose you notice a peer crossing their arms and furrowing their brow during a discussion. By interpreting these signs of disagreement, you can adjust your approach. This might mean you ask probing questions to learn more about what they're thinking. Or, it might mean you choose a more collaborative discussion style. Without noticing their body language, you would have kept your approach the exact same, despite their disagreement.

For Home Life

At home, as a parent or spouse, being able to read facial expressions can help you to be more proactive in your support of loved ones. Imagine your child comes home from school looking upset but doesn't want to talk about it. By observing their facial expressions and body language, you might sense their need for comfort and reassurance. You could choose to sit with them, offering your calming presence and support, without demanding to learn more about how they're feeling.

TAKE ACTION: This week, watch a movie with the sound off and focus on interpreting the emotions through facial expressions and body language.

SoA8. Grow Your Cultural Sensitivity

Seek to educate yourself about different cultural norms. Ask your colleagues about their traditions. This activity isn't about formal training or workshops. Instead, it's about everyday mindfulness and empathy.

How to Do It

1. Educate Yourself: Research important holidays and traditions of cultures that are different from your own.
2. Acknowledge and Respect: Recognize and respect these events in your interactions and scheduling.
3. Stay Informed: Be aware of newsworthy events that might impact colleagues or family members from different cultural backgrounds.
4. Adapt Communication: Adjust your communication style to be more inclusive and considerate of different social dynamics.
5. Foster Discussions: Encourage open discussions about cultural traditions and current events at work and at home.
6. Show Empathy: Offer support and show empathy towards those affected by significant cultural or global events.

For Managers

As a manager, cultural sensitivity can significantly enhance your leadership. On a team that includes employees from various cultural backgrounds, you need to be aware of and acknowledge everyone. For example, when a holiday, like Diwali or Ramadan, is approaching for some team members, your acknowledgment and flexibility will show respect and support for their traditions.

For Individual Contributors

For team members, cultural sensitivity can improve your flexibility around collaboration and communication. For example, if you work in a global organization, you may collaborate with a colleague from Japan, where business etiquette and communication styles differ from Western norms. You might notice that your Japanese colleague tends to be more reserved in meetings and values group harmony over individual opinions. By observing this pattern, you can adapt your approach to be a better collaborator. You might seek their input privately before meetings and ensure that your communication is more collaborative.

For Home Life

At home, as a parent or spouse, cultural sensitivity can deepen relationships and instill a sense of respect and appreciation for diversity. During family conversations, discussing different cultural traditions and current global events can foster empathy and understanding. For instance, you might have a spouse who is deeply affected by news from their home country. By acknowledging and showing concern for these events, you can offer emotional support and deepen your relationship. Similarly, you can teach your children about cultural holidays.

TAKE ACTION: This week, learn about an upcoming cultural holiday and acknowledge it in your interactions with colleagues or family members.

SoA9. Practice Perspective-Taking

Imagine you are in a meeting and a colleague proposes an idea that you initially disagree with. Instead of dismissing it outright, you make a conscious effort to see the situation from their viewpoint. That's the basic idea behind perspective-taking. This activity isn't about agreeing with everyone about everything. It's about understanding the motivations and feelings behind different perspectives.

How to Do It

1. Pause and Reflect: When faced with a differing opinion or conflict, take a moment to pause and reflect before responding.
2. Ask Questions: Engage in open-ended questions to understand the other person's viewpoint.
3. Listen Actively: Pay close attention to their words and body language without interrupting.
4. Acknowledge Feelings: Validate their emotions and perspectives, even if you don't agree.
5. Consider Motivations: Try to understand the underlying motivations and reasons behind their viewpoint.
6. Communicate Empathetically: Respond with empathy, showing that you respect and value their perspective.

For Managers

As a manager, perspective-taking can transform potential conflict into constructive dialogue. Suppose a team member consistently resists a new process you've implemented. Instead of becoming frustrated, take a moment to understand their viewpoint. Perhaps they feel the new process overlooks crucial steps that ensure quality. By acknowledging their concerns and discussing possible adjustments, you not only validate their feelings but also improve the process with their insights.

For Individual Contributors

For an individual contributor, seeing things from a colleague's perspective can help build mutual understanding. Imagine working on a project with a peer who always seems to have a different approach than you. By making an effort to understand their way of doing things, you might discover new methods that enhance the project's outcome. You may even adopt elements of their approach in the future. For example, if they prefer detailed planning while you lean towards flexibility, recognizing the value in their thoroughness can help balance your strategy. On the other hand, if you had resisted their way of thinking, it may have resulted in a conflict or a weaker collaboration.

For Home Life

At home, as a parent or spouse, perspective-taking can build empathy and deepen trust. Consider a situation where your child is upset about a decision you've made. Instead of enforcing the decision without explanation, try to understand their feelings and viewpoints. Maybe they feel excluded from the decision-making process or fear your decision's impact on their daily routine. With this in mind, you might open up a conversation to better understand their perspective. As a result, you may even be able to address their concerns and find a compromise.

TAKE ACTION: This week, practice perspective-taking by engaging in a conversation with a colleague or family member about a topic you disagree on.

SoA10. Note Introverted and Extroverted Traits

Observe how your colleagues interact during meetings and social events. Notice who tends to speak up and who remains quiet, and consider how these behaviors might relate to their introverted or extroverted tendencies. This activity isn't about categorizing people. It's about understanding and respecting their different ways of engaging with the world.

How to Do It

1. Observe Interactions: Pay attention to how people engage in meetings and social settings.
2. Identify Preferences: Notice who prefers speaking up and who tends to stay quiet.
3. Create Opportunities: Provide multiple ways for people to share their ideas, respecting both introverted and extroverted preferences.
4. Respect Differences: Understand that introverts may prefer written communication or one-on-one discussions, while extroverts may need to verbalize their thoughts.
5. Balance Needs: At home and work, find activities that cater to both introverted and extroverted tendencies.
6. Communicate Empathetically: Show appreciation for each person's unique way of interacting and processing information.

For Managers

As a manager, recognizing and respecting personality traits can help you harness the strengths of each personality type and foster a more inclusive environment. Suppose you have an introverted team member who rarely speaks up in meetings. Instead of assuming they have nothing to contribute, create opportunities for them to share their ideas in ways that suit their comfort level, such as one-on-one discussions or written feedback. Conversely, understand that extroverted team members might need to talk through their ideas and may change their opinions after processing them aloud. For instance, an extroverted employee might dominate a brainstorming session, but their initial ideas might evolve significantly.

For Individual Contributors

For an individual contributor, understanding introvert-extrovert dynamics can improve your interactions with your colleagues. If you notice a colleague who is quieter during meetings, take the initiative to ask for their input in smaller settings or through written communication. This approach shows respect for their preferences and can reveal valuable insights that might otherwise be overlooked. On the other hand, if you work with an extroverted colleague who frequently vocalizes their thoughts, be patient with their process of speaking and thinking. Encourage them by actively listening and acknowledging their need for verbal processing.

For Home Life

At home, recognizing introverted and extroverted tendencies can help you understand and interact with your family members. Suppose your spouse is introverted and often declines social invitations, preferring quiet evenings at home. Instead of feeling rejected or pressured to socialize, understand that this is how they recharge. Plan activities that align with their preferences, such as a cozy movie night or a quiet dinner. For extroverted family members, like a child who thrives on social interactions, ensure they have opportunities to connect with friends and engage in group activities.

TAKE ACTION: This week, create a balanced opportunity for both introverted and extroverted colleagues to share their ideas in your next team meeting.

SoA11. Observe and Understand People's Goals & Motivations

Take a moment to observe and understand what drives the people around you. This activity isn't about judging others but about gaining insights into their motivations and goals. Who is striving for a promotion? Who values job stability and the flexibility to pick up their kids after school? Who is motivated by money, and who wants to make a significant impact on the world?

How to Do It

1. Observe and Listen: Pay attention to what colleagues, family, and friends prioritize in conversations and actions.
2. Ask Questions: Engage in open-ended questions to learn about their goals and motivations.
3. Acknowledge Differences: Recognize and respect that different people have different drivers.
4. Provide Support: Tailor your support to align with their goals, whether it's career development, work-life balance, or social impact.
5. Communicate Effectively: Use this understanding to enhance your communication and collaboration efforts.
6. Reflect and Adapt: Regularly reflect on these insights and adapt your approach as needed to maintain alignment with their evolving goals.

For Managers

As a manager, understanding your team members' goals and

motivations can help you demonstrate empathy and respect for personal goals. For instance, you might have an employee who is highly motivated by career advancement and consistently takes on challenging projects. Recognizing this, you can provide them with opportunities for professional development and mentorship, which can lead to greater job satisfaction and retention. Conversely, another team member might prioritize work-life balance to spend time with their family. By supporting their need for flexible hours or remote work options, you'll help keep this employee engaged.

For Individual Contributors

For an individual contributor, understanding your colleagues' motivations can help you influence without authority. Suppose you notice a coworker who seems highly focused on financial rewards. By acknowledging this, you can tailor your interactions to highlight how successful project outcomes might lead to bonuses or raises, aligning your collaborative efforts with their goals. On the other hand, if you work with someone passionate about making a positive social impact, you can support their initiatives and find common ground in projects that align with both your goals.

For Home Life

At home, understanding the goals and motivations of your spouse or children allows you to provide the right support and encouragement, fostering their growth and happiness. For example, your spouse might be driven by a desire to make a meaningful difference in their community through volunteer work. By recognizing and supporting their commitment, you can offer encouragement and practical help, such as managing household responsibilities to free up their time.

TAKE ACTION: This week, ask a colleague about their professional goals and think of one way you can support them in achieving these goals.

SoA12. Ask Power Questions

Instead of closed-ended or simple questions, use powerful open-ended questions to invite meaningful conversations and provide insights into the other person's motivations, experiences, and interests. When you first meet someone, try asking powerful open-ended questions like, "How did you get into your line of work?" or "What do you like to do for fun when you're not working?" or "What's been the best and worst part of your week?"

How to Do It

Choose the Right Moment: Find a relaxed and appropriate time to ask your power questions, whether it's during a meeting, a break, or a family dinner.

Ask Open-Ended Questions: Formulate questions that require more than a yes or no answer to encourage detailed responses. Refer to the ten examples later in this strategy for inspiration.

Listen Actively: Pay close attention to the answers, showing genuine interest and engagement.

Follow Up: Ask follow-up questions based on their responses to delve deeper and show that you value their perspective.

Share Your Own Experiences: Create a balanced conversation by sharing your own relevant experiences and thoughts.

Reflect on Insights: Use the insights gained from these conversations to better understand and support the people around you.

For Managers

As a manager, asking power questions can help you offer targeted support and recognition, which can boost their morale and productivity. For instance, during a one-on-one meeting with a team member, you might ask, "What's been the most rewarding and challenging part of your current project?" This question encourages your employees to share their achievements and difficulties, giving you a deeper understanding of their work experience.

For Individual Contributors

As an individual contributor, asking power questions can help you learn about and appreciate your teammates' motivations, passions, and expertise. In turn, this can help you find new ways to collaborate. Suppose you're working on a cross-departmental project and you meet a new colleague. Asking them, "How did you get into your field?" can uncover shared interests or complementary skills. For example, you might learn that they transitioned from a completely different industry and can offer a unique perspective to the project.

For Home Life

At home, asking power questions can improve communication and create an environment where everyone feels heard and appreciated. For instance, asking your spouse, "What's been the highlight and lowlight of your week?" opens up space for sharing experiences and emotions. This can lead to meaningful conversations that strengthen your emotional bond. Similarly, asking your children questions like, "What do you like to do for fun when you're not at school?" can help you understand their interests and support their passions.

Here are ten examples of power questions:

"What are you trying to achieve?" This question clarifies the ultimate goal, helping to align efforts and focus on desired outcomes.

"What would success look like?" It prompts visualization of the end result, making it easier to create actionable steps towards achieving it.

"What is the biggest challenge you're facing right now?" Identifying the primary obstacle allows for targeted problem-solving and resource allocation.

"What options have you considered so far?" This question explores the range of potential solutions, encouraging creativity and comprehensive thinking.

"What's holding you back from moving forward?" It helps identify internal or external barriers, providing insight into potential areas for intervention.

"What would you do if you knew you couldn't fail?" Encourages bold thinking and risk-taking by removing the fear of failure from the equation.

"Who else is affected by this decision?" Considers the broader impact of decisions, promoting empathy and stakeholder awareness.

"What's the worst that could happen?" Helps assess the real risks involved, often diminishing irrational fears and clarifying manageable risks.

"What resources do you need to achieve your goal?" Focuses on identifying and securing necessary support and tools to ensure preparedness.

"How will you measure success?" Establishes clear metrics for progress and achievement, promoting accountability and continuous improvement.

TAKE ACTION: This week, ask a colleague or family member a powerful open-ended question to spark a meaningful conversation.

SoA13. Scan the Energy of the Room

When you enter a room, take a moment to observe the atmosphere and the interactions taking place. Notice the energy levels, who is engaging with whom, and the overall mood of the group. This activity is about tuning into the unspoken dynamics that influence social interactions.

How to Do It
1. Pause and Observe: When entering a room, take a moment to observe the interactions and overall mood.
2. Notice Body Language: Pay attention to non-verbal cues like body language and facial expressions.
3. Identify Energy Levels: Assess whether the energy is high, low, tense, or relaxed.
4. Engage with Open-Ended Questions: Initiate conversations with questions that encourage detailed responses.
5. Balance Participation: Encourage quieter individuals to share their thoughts and manage dominant voices.
6. Respond with Empathy: Address any negative energy with empathetic and supportive responses.

For Managers
As a manager, scanning the energy of the room can lead to more productive and harmonious meetings. For example, during a team meeting, you might notice some team members are unusually quiet while others dominate the conversation. By recognizing this imbalance, you can address it directly by encouraging quieter members to share their thoughts. This can be done by asking open-ended questions like, "What

do you think about this idea?" or "How did you approach similar challenges in the past?" By engaging with these team members, you may learn more about why their mood is different (more quiet than usual). This enables you to adapt your approach to better meet their needs.

For Individual Contributors

For an individual contributor, understanding the energy in the room can improve your ability to communicate in a timely, context-appropriate way. Imagine you are in a cross-functional project kickoff meeting, and you sense tension or discomfort among the group. By acknowledging this, you can take steps to ease the atmosphere. You might initiate a casual conversation with a question like, "What do you like to do for fun when you're not working?" This can break the ice and build rapport, making it easier for everyone to collaborate effectively throughout the meeting.

For Home Life

At home, scanning the energy of the room can help foster a nurturing and understanding home environment. For instance, if you come home and notice your spouse seems stressed or your child appears withdrawn, take the time to ask empathetic questions such as, "What's been the best and worst part of your day?" This can open up meaningful conversations and provide insights into their current emotional state.

TAKE ACTION: This week, when you enter a meeting or a family gathering, take a moment to scan the energy and ask an open-ended question to engage with those around you.

RELATIONSHIP MANAGEMENT STRATEGIES

Building and maintaining strong relationships is at the heart of emotional intelligence, and relationship management is key to achieving this goal. Relationship management involves the ability to inspire, influence, and develop others while managing conflict and fostering collaboration. This skill is essential for effective leadership, teamwork, and personal connections.

This chapter will provide you with a comprehensive set of practical approaches to help you navigate interpersonal dynamics, resolve conflicts constructively, and cultivate lasting, positive relationships.

1. **Use Empathetic Echoing to Show You're Listening:** Actively listen to someone and reflect back their sentiments in your own words, helping them feel understood and valued.
2. **Show That You Care:** Express that you care for at least three different people in your life to enhance your relationships.
3. **Resolve Conflicts with the S.A.M. Model:** In your next conflict, use the S.A.M. model to engage in constructive conversations and work through your conflict.

4. **Check in Consistently:** Periodically check in on the emotional well-being of your team, family, or partner.

5. **Offer Constructive Feedback:** Practice giving constructive feedback that is specific, non-judgmental, and oriented towards finding a solution.

6. **Give Recognition (e.g., Say Thanks):** Take time to recognize others' achievements and say thank you.

7. **Be Inclusive:** Make a conscious effort to include a colleague, team member, or family member in a discussion.

8. **Share Credit:** Share success and credit with your team or partner.

9. **Celebrate the Accomplishments of Others:** This week, celebrate a colleague or family member's milestone or achievement. Consider events like birthdays, work anniversaries, and wins of favorite sports teams.

10. **Accept Feedback Gracefully:** Seek out and accept feedback from a colleague, team member, or family member. Focus on being receptive, curious, and growth-minded, not defensive.

11. **Paint a Picture of a Bright Future:** Share a compelling future vision with your team, peers, or family to motivate, inspire, and align your group.

12. **Foster Psychological Safety:** This week, make a point of inviting in and valuing the input of your team members, peers, or family members.

13. **Be Humble:** Practice humility by sharing credit for success with a colleague or family member.

RM1. Use Empathetic Echoing to Show You're Listening

Empathetic Echoing is a powerful tool for enhancing your interactions and relationships by mirroring the emotions and feelings expressed by others. This practice involves actively listening to someone and reflecting back their sentiments in your own words, helping them feel understood and valued.

How to Do It
1. Listen Actively: Pay full attention to the speaker without interrupting. Focus on their words, tone, and body language.
2. Reflect Emotions: Identify the primary emotion the speaker is expressing. This could be joy, frustration, sadness, or excitement.
3. Echo Back: Use your own words to reflect their feelings. For example, "It sounds like you're feeling excited about the new project."
4. Validate and Support: Show that you understand and acknowledge their feelings. Offer your support if appropriate.
5. Stay Neutral: Avoid inserting your own opinions or solutions unless asked. The goal is to make the speaker feel heard and understood.

For Managers
As a manager, using Empathetic Echoing in one-on-one meetings can foster a more supportive and transparent work environment. For instance, during a performance review, if an employee expresses frustration about their workload, you

might say, "It sounds like you're feeling overwhelmed with your current tasks." This acknowledgment not only validates their feelings but also opens the door for a constructive conversation about potential solutions.

For Individual Contributors

For team members, Empathetic Echoing is a powerful way to build trust and camaraderie within your team, making collective tasks more manageable and enjoyable. Imagine you're in a team meeting, and a colleague voices concern about a looming deadline. You could respond with, "I hear that you're worried about meeting the deadline. I also have concerns." Or, "I hear that you aren't sure about this deadline, and here is why I think we'll be OK." This simple reflection shows empathy and can defuse tension, encouraging a more cooperative approach to problem-solving.

For Home Life

At home, Empathetic Echoing can create a more harmonious and understanding household, fostering deeper connections and emotional resilience. As a parent or spouse, it's crucial to acknowledge the emotions of your loved ones. For example, if your child is upset about a conflict with a friend, you might say, "It seems like you're really hurt by what happened." This validation helps them process their emotions and reassures them of your support. In this way, you can also help your child expand their emotional vocabulary.

TAKE ACTION: This week, practice Empathetic Echoing in at least three conversations to enhance your relationships.

RM2. Show That You Care

Showing genuine care and concern for others can profoundly impact your relationships. This simple yet powerful practice involves actively demonstrating empathy, understanding, and support for those around you.

How to Do It

1. Listen Actively: Pay full attention to the person speaking without interrupting. Show that you are genuinely interested in what they have to say.
2. Acknowledge Feelings: Recognize and validate their emotions. You can say, "I can see that you're feeling [emotion]."
3. Offer Support: Ask how you can help or provide assistance. Be specific in your offers, such as, "Can I help with [task]?"
4. Follow Through: Ensure that you follow up on your offers of help. Consistency is key to building trust.
5. Express Gratitude: Show appreciation for the person and their efforts. A simple thank you can go a long way.

For Managers

As a manager, demonstrating that you care about your employees during regular check-ins or casual conversations can lead to a more motivated and loyal team. For example, you could routinely ask about their workload and stress levels. If you know that they are going through a tough family issue–whether sick kids or caring for an aging parent–you could offer sympathy or even some time off. This shows that you value them as individuals and helps foster a team culture of empathy and trust.

For Individual Contributors

For team members, showing care can be as simple as asking colleagues about their weekend or any personal activities they've been involved in. For instance, on a Monday morning, you might ask, "How was your weekend? Did you do anything fun?" This shows genuine interest in their lives outside of work and helps build stronger personal connections. Regularly engaging in these conversations can create a more friendly and cohesive team environment where colleagues feel valued as individuals.

For Home Life

At home, regularly expressing your care and support can lead to stronger, more resilient family relationships. For instance, if your partner is feeling overwhelmed with household chores or has to work late, you could say, "I see this is a tough day. Let me take care of dinner tonight." This helps alleviate their burden and reinforces your partnership.

TAKE ACTION: This week, show genuine care for three different people in your life to enhance your relationships.

RM3. Resolve Conflicts with the S.A.M. Model

Engaging in constructive conversations to resolve conflicts can transform your relationships. Conflicts often get put off or avoided because they are emotionally charged, but recognizing that conflict is a normal part of life can help you navigate through them more effectively. The S.A.M. model is a simple yet powerful framework:

- <u>S</u>ay your side of the situation.
- <u>A</u>sk about their side of the conflict.
- <u>M</u>utually agree on a path forward.

How to Do It:

1. Identify the Conflict: Recognize the conflict and the emotions involved.
2. Set a Meeting Time: Choose a time when all parties can discuss the issue without distractions.
3. Say Your Side: Clearly express your perspective and feelings without blaming others.
4. Ask for Their Side: Invite the other party to share their viewpoint and listen actively without interrupting.
5. Mutually Agree: Collaborate to find a solution that addresses both sides' concerns and agree on the path forward.
6. Follow Up: Set a follow-up meeting to ensure the agreement is being honored and to address any ongoing issues.

For Managers

As a manager, resolving conflicts is a critical skill. Imagine a situation where two team members disagree on the direction of a project. Schedule a meeting with both parties and use the S.A.M. model. Start by clearly stating your perspective on the situation and acknowledging any emotions involved. Next, invite each team member to share their viewpoints. Listen actively as they share. Finally, guide the conversation toward finding a mutual agreement on how to proceed. For instance, if one team member feels undervalued and another is frustrated with deadlines, agreeing on a realistic timeline that addresses both concerns can help resolve the conflict.

For Individual Contributors

As an individual contributor, working with peers often involves navigating conflicts to maintain a harmonious work environment. Suppose you have a disagreement with a colleague over task responsibilities. Begin by expressing your side—why you believe the task allocation is unfair or unbalanced. Then, ask for their perspective to understand their concerns or limitations. By fostering an open dialogue, you can mutually agree on redistributing tasks in a way that leverages each person's strengths and workload capacity. Resolving conflicts like this often feels challenging and draining in the short term, but in the long term, these conflicts strengthen your working relationships.

For Home Life

At home, whether as a parent or a spouse, conflicts can arise from daily stressors and misunderstandings. Picture a scenario where there is a disagreement about household chores.

Use the S.A.M. model to address this. Start by calmly explaining your view and the emotions you're experiencing, such as feeling overwhelmed. Then, ask your partner or children for their side, encouraging them to share their feelings and perspectives. Through this empathetic exchange, you can come to a mutual agreement, such as creating a fair chore schedule that everyone commits to. This not only resolves the conflict but also fosters a sense of teamwork and understanding.

TAKE ACTION: This week, use the S.A.M. model to resolve a conflict in your personal or professional life, enhancing your relationship management skills.

RM4. Check In Consistently

Regularly checking in with people can significantly enhance your relationships. This simple activity involves taking a few moments to connect with others, understanding their current state, and showing genuine interest in their well-being.

How to Do It:

1. Schedule Regular Check-Ins: Set aside specific times for regular check-ins with team members, peers, or family.

2. Ask Open-Ended Questions: Use questions that encourage sharing, such as "How are you feeling?" or "Is there anything on your mind?" "What was the best and worst part of your day/week?"

3. Listen Actively: Pay attention to their responses without interrupting and show that you value their feelings and perspectives.

4. Show Empathy: Acknowledge their emotions and offer support or solutions where appropriate.

5. Follow Up: Revisit previous conversations to show that you remember and care about their ongoing well-being.

6. Be Consistent: Make check-ins a regular part of your routine to build trust and strengthen relationships over time.

For Managers

As a manager, consistently checking in with your team can help improve morale and productivity, fostering a more supportive work environment. Schedule weekly or bi-weekly one-on-one meetings with each team member, even if they are brief. Use this check-in time to ask how they are doing and if there is anything they need support with. By creating a space for open communication, you might uncover underlying issues like stress from an impending deadline or personal challenges.

For Individual Contributors

As an individual contributor, checking in with your peers can build trust and camaraderie. Suppose you are working on a project with a colleague and notice they seem overwhelmed. Taking the initiative to ask how they are doing and to see if they need help can go a long way. For instance, you might offer to share tasks or brainstorm solutions together to help alleviate their stress and improve the project's outcome.

For Home Life

At home, checking in with family members fosters a nurturing and understanding family environment. Consider creating rituals to "check in." This could be a nightly dinner at the table (with smartphones put away!) or a weekly date night. With children, for example, you might regularly ask them how they are feeling about school or their friends. This can help you stay attuned to their emotional needs.

TAKE ACTION: This week, schedule regular check-ins with your team, peers, or family to enhance your relationship management skills.

RM5. Offer Constructive Feedback

Offering constructive feedback is an essential activity to enhance relationships and foster growth in various aspects of life. This practice involves providing feedback in a way that is helpful and supportive rather than critical or damaging. The B.I.G. model (Behavior, Impact, Get Agreement) is an effective approach to ensure feedback is clear and constructive.

How to Do It:
1. Prepare Your Feedback: Think about the specific behaviors or outcomes you want to address.
2. Choose the Right Time and Place: Ensure privacy and a comfortable setting to discuss feedback.
3. Be Specific: Focus on particular instances rather than general behavior.
4. Use "I" Statements: Frame your feedback from your perspective to avoid sounding accusatory.
5. Follow the B.I.G. Model:
- Behavior: Mention the specific behavior.
- Impact: Explain the impact it's having.
- Get Agreement: Get agreement about their understanding and any next steps.
6. Invite Dialogue: Encourage the other person to share their thoughts and feelings about your feedback.
7. Follow Up: Check in later to see how the person is doing and if any improvements have been made.

For Managers
As a manager, offering constructive feedback can help your team members improve without growing discouraged or

unmotivated. Schedule regular feedback sessions with your team members, focusing on specific behaviors and outcomes. For example, if a team member's presentation lacked clarity, you might say, "I noticed that in your last presentation, some points were unclear (Behavior). This made it difficult for the team to understand the key messages and delayed decision-making (Impact). Do you agree that we could benefit from a more structured approach with clear visuals? How do you feel about working on this together (Get Agreement)?"

For Individual Contributors

As an individual contributor, giving and receiving feedback from peers can show them you care about their perspective and want to collaborate on a solution. Suppose a colleague constantly misses deadlines, impacting your work. Approach them with empathy, saying, "I've noticed that the project deadlines have been missed a few times (Behavior). This has rippled into my own planning, and I had to work over the weekend to get us back on track (Impact). Can we discuss ways to better manage our timelines? For example, the earlier I know you'll need extra time, the easier it will be for me to rearrange my schedule (Get Agreement)."

For Home Life

At home, whether as a parent or a spouse, constructive feedback can support personal growth. Imagine your child is struggling with their homework and becoming frustrated. Instead of criticizing, you could say, "I see that you're having difficulty with your assignment (Behavior). This seems to be making you very frustrated and unhappy (Impact). Can we agree to break it down into smaller parts and work through it together? Does that sound good to you (Get Agreement)?" This feedback not only offers a solution but also shows your support and willingness to help.

TAKE ACTION: This week, use the B.I.G. model to offer constructive feedback to a colleague, team member, or family member to enhance your relationship management skills.

RM6. Give Recognition (e.g., Say Thanks)

Expressing gratitude and giving recognition is a simple yet powerful way to strengthen relationships and foster a positive environment. This practice involves acknowledging the efforts and contributions of others, showing appreciation for their hard work, and saying thanks.

How to Do It:
1. Identify the Effort: Look for actions or behaviors that deserve recognition.
2. Be Specific: Clearly mention what you are thanking the person for.
3. Express Sincerely: Ensure your gratitude is genuine and heartfelt.
4. Public or Private: Decide whether to give recognition publicly or privately, based on the situation and the person's preference.
5. Be Timely: Offer your thanks soon after the event or action you are recognizing.
6. Follow Up: Occasionally check in and continue to show appreciation to reinforce positive behaviors.

For Managers
As a manager, giving recognition is crucial for motivating your team and building a supportive work culture. Regularly acknowledge your team members' efforts and achievements. For example, if a team member successfully completes a challenging project, you might say, "Thank you for your hard work on the recent project. Your dedication and attention to

detail made a significant impact on our success." By expressing your gratitude, you not only boost their morale but also reinforce positive behaviors, encouraging them to continue performing at their best.

For Individual Contributors

As an individual contributor, recognizing your peers can strengthen your working relationships and show that you're a team player. Suppose a colleague went out of their way to help you meet a tight deadline. Take a moment to say, "I really appreciate your assistance with the report last week. Your support helped me meet the deadline, and I couldn't have done it without you." If it makes sense, recognize their contribution in a public setting and give them credit in front of your team and boss.

For Home Life

At home, expressing gratitude to your family members can significantly improve your relationships. Saying thanks for everyday efforts can make a big difference. Imagine your partner cooked dinner after a long day. You could say, "Thank you for making dinner tonight. It really means a lot to me and gives me a chance to relax." Similarly, with your children, recognizing their efforts, such as completing chores or doing well in school, can encourage positive behaviors and build their self-esteem. For example, "Thank you for helping with the dishes tonight. Your help made the evening so much smoother."

TAKE ACTION: This week, say thanks to a colleague, team member, or family member for their efforts to strengthen your relationship management skills.

RM7. Be Inclusive

Including others in discussions, decisions, and activities is a powerful way to strengthen relationships and foster a sense of belonging. This practice involves actively seeking out and valuing the input and participation of everyone involved.

How to Do It:

1. Make a Conscious Effort: Actively seek to include others in discussions and decisions.
2. Ask for Input: Directly ask for opinions and ideas from everyone involved.
3. Listen Actively: Pay attention to what others are saying and show that you value their input.
4. Encourage Participation: Create opportunities for everyone to share their thoughts and ideas.
5. Acknowledge Contributions: Recognize and appreciate the input of others.
6. Follow Through: Ensure that the input received is considered and acted upon where appropriate.
7. Create a Safe Space: Foster an environment where everyone feels comfortable sharing their thoughts.

For Managers

As a manager, fostering an inclusive environment shows that you value each team member's input and leads to more creative and innovative ideas. During meetings, make it a point to call on different team members to share their perspectives. For example, you might say, "I'd like to hear from everyone on this topic. Maria, what are your thoughts on our current marketing strategy?"

For Individual Contributors

As an individual contributor, promoting inclusivity among peers can encourage participation from more perspectives, leading to stronger working relationships and better project outcomes. Suppose you are working on a project and notice that a colleague has been quiet during brainstorming sessions. Take the initiative to ask for their input by saying, "John, I'd love to hear your ideas on this. You always have great insights."

For Home Life

At home, actively seeking the opinions and ideas of your family members can make a big difference. Imagine planning a family vacation. Instead of making all the decisions yourself, you could say, "I'd love to hear everyone's ideas for our vacation. Where would you like to go, and what activities should we include?" This approach ensures that everyone feels involved and that their preferences are considered.

TAKE ACTION: This week, make a conscious effort to include a colleague, team member, or family member in a discussion or decision.

RM8. Share Credit

Acknowledging and sharing credit for successes is a vital activity to strengthen relationships and build a positive environment. This practice involves recognizing the contributions of others, celebrating team achievements, and ensuring everyone feels valued for their efforts.

How to Do It:

1. Be Observant: Pay attention to the contributions and efforts of those around you.
2. Acknowledge Specific Contributions: Clearly mention what each person did to contribute to the success.
3. Be Sincere: Ensure your recognition is genuine and heartfelt.
4. Publicly or Privately: Decide whether to give credit publicly or privately based on the situation and the person's preference.
5. Be Timely: Acknowledge contributions soon after the achievement or success.
6. Encourage Peer Recognition: Foster an environment where team members also recognize each other's efforts.
7. Celebrate as a Team: Organize small celebrations or acknowledgments to collectively appreciate the team's success.

For Managers

As a manager, sharing credit can boost morale and encourage continued collaboration and dedication. For instance, after a successful project, take the time during a team meeting to highlight individual contributions. You might say, "I want to thank everyone for their hard work on this project. Sarah's innovative ideas and John's attention to detail were crucial to our success."

For Individual Contributors

As an individual contributor, giving credit to peers shows your appreciation and fosters a culture where everyone feels valued and motivated to contribute their best. Suppose you worked on a project with a colleague, and it turned out to be a great success. During a team meeting, you could say, "I want to acknowledge how much Tom's insights contributed to our project's success. His feedback was invaluable." Highlight specific examples and behaviors to bring their contribution to life.

For Home Life

At home, sharing credit with family members fosters a sense of teamwork and appreciation within the family, encouraging everyone to continue contributing positively. For example, after a successful family event like a dinner party, you might say to your partner, "I really appreciate how much effort everyone put into making this evening special. The kids did a great job setting the table, and your cooking was amazing."

TAKE ACTION: This week, make a conscious effort to share credit with a colleague, team member, or family member.

RM9. Celebrate the Accomplishments of Others

Celebrating milestones and achievements is a powerful way to strengthen relationships and foster a positive environment. This practice involves recognizing and celebrating important events such as birthdays, work anniversaries, or personal achievements like completing a 10K race.

How to Do It:

1. Keep Track of Important Dates: Maintain a calendar of birthdays, work anniversaries, and personal achievements.
2. Acknowledge Publicly: Recognize the milestone or achievement in front of others, whether in a meeting or a family gathering.
3. Be Specific: Mention the details of what you are celebrating and why it is significant.
4. Organize a Small Celebration: Arrange for a cake, a card, or a small gift to mark the occasion.
5. Express Genuine Appreciation: Ensure your recognition is heartfelt and sincere.
6. Encourage Others to Join: Invite colleagues or family members to participate in the celebration.
7. Follow Up: Continue to show appreciation and support for the person's ongoing efforts and achievements.

For Managers

As a manager, organizing a small celebration or giving a token of appreciation can make your team feel valued and appreciated, enhancing their commitment and productivity.

For instance, you can acknowledge work anniversaries during team meetings. If a team member reaches a five-year milestone, you might say, "Today we're celebrating Julia's five-year anniversary with our company. Her dedication and hard work have been invaluable to our success."

For Individual Contributors

As an individual contributor, celebrating your peers' achievements helps foster a sense of camaraderie and mutual respect. Suppose a colleague has just completed a significant project or achieved a personal milestone, like running a marathon. Take the initiative to congratulate them during a team huddle, saying, "I want to take a moment to recognize Mike for completing his first marathon last weekend. That's an incredible achievement!"

For Home Life

At home, celebrating the achievements and special occasions of family members shows you care and creates lasting memories. For example, if your child wins an award at school, you could say, "We're so proud of you for winning the science fair. Let's have a special dinner to celebrate your hard work."

TAKE ACTION: This week, celebrate a colleague, team member, or family member's milestone or achievement to strengthen your relationship management skills.

RM10. Accept Feedback Gracefully

Receiving criticism and constructive feedback is an essential activity that can significantly enhance your personal and professional relationships. By accepting feedback gracefully and graciously, you can turn potentially negative situations into opportunities for growth and improvement.

How to Do It:

1. Stay Calm: Take a deep breath and maintain your composure when receiving feedback.
2. Listen Actively: Pay attention to the feedback without interrupting or becoming defensive.
3. Acknowledge the Feedback: Show that you understand the feedback and appreciate the person's perspective.
4. Ask for Clarification: If needed, ask for specific examples or suggestions to better understand the feedback.
5. Reflect on the Feedback: Take time to consider the feedback and how you can apply it.
6. Respond Positively: Express gratitude for the feedback and outline any steps you will take to improve. Even if you end up disagreeing with the feedback you can still thank the person for sharing their thoughts and let them know you'll think about it.
7. Follow Through: Implement the feedback and make visible efforts to improve based on the suggestions received.

For Managers

As a manager, demonstrating the ability to accept feedback

gracefully sets a powerful example for your team. Imagine receiving feedback from your team about your communication style during meetings. Instead of becoming defensive, you might say, "Thank you for bringing this to my attention. I understand that clearer communication is important, and I will work on being more concise and direct in our future meetings. Do you have any specific suggestions on how I can improve?" This approach shows your willingness to grow and fosters a team culture of openness and continuous improvement.

For Individual Contributors

As an individual contributor, accepting feedback from peers is one of the fastest ways to grow your skills and build trust with your teammates. Suppose a colleague points out that your recent report lacked detail. A good response should demonstrate your commitment to quality work and collaboration. For instance, you might say, "I appreciate your feedback and will make sure to include more comprehensive data in future reports. Could you help me identify which areas need more detail?"

For Home Life

At home, accepting constructive feedback shows your willingness to listen and improve, reinforcing your commitment to maintaining a supportive and cooperative household. For example, if your spouse mentions that you often leave tasks unfinished around the house, you could respond with, "I hear you and understand that it's frustrating. I will make a conscious effort to complete my tasks. Could you help me by reminding me when I overlook something?"

TAKE ACTION: This week, actively seek and gracefully accept constructive feedback from a colleague, team member, or family member to strengthen your relationship management skills.

RM11. Paint a Picture of a Bright Future

Painting a compelling future vision is an essential activity to inspire and motivate those around you. This practice involves articulating a clear and positive vision of the future that can guide and energize your team, peers, and family.

How to Do It:

1. Define the Vision: Clearly articulate what the future looks like and why it is desirable.
2. Connect to Values: Ensure the vision aligns with the values and aspirations of your audience.
3. Be Specific: Provide detailed and vivid descriptions to make the vision tangible.
4. Communicate Regularly: Keep the vision at the forefront through regular communication and updates.
5. Involve Others: Encourage feedback and input to refine and strengthen the vision.
6. Demonstrate Commitment: Show your dedication to the vision through your actions and decisions.
7. Celebrate Milestones: Recognize and celebrate progress towards the vision to maintain momentum.

For Managers

As a manager, offering a compelling vision helps team members see the bigger picture and their role in achieving it, fostering a sense of purpose and unity. Imagine leading a team through a major project. By sharing a vivid picture of the project's successful completion, you might say, "Imagine how our clients will benefit from our new software, increasing their efficiency and satisfaction. Our team will be recognized as innovators, setting a new industry standard." This vision provides a clear goal and ignites enthusiasm and dedication.

For Individual Contributors

As an individual contributor, aligning your vision with your peers can help you and your team see the long-term benefits of their current efforts, increasing your commitment and collaboration. Suppose your team is working on a challenging deadline. You could inspire your colleagues by saying, "If we can pull together and meet this deadline, we'll demonstrate our capability to handle high-pressure situations and secure more high-profile projects in the future. This will be a significant step in our careers and for our department's reputation."

For Home Life

At home, sharing a compelling future vision aligns everyone's efforts toward common goals. Whether planning a family project or discussing long-term plans, painting a positive picture of the future is powerful. For instance, you might say, "Imagine in a few years, we'll have saved enough for that dream vacation, where we can all relax and explore new cultures together. Working together to save now will make that trip all the more rewarding."

TAKE ACTION: This week, share a compelling future vision with your team, peers, or family to motivate, inspire, and align your group.

RM12. Foster Psychological Safety

Creating an environment where individuals feel safe to express their ideas and concerns without fear of retribution is crucial for building strong relationships and fostering innovation. This practice, known as fostering psychological safety, encourages open communication and mutual respect.

How to Do It:

1. Listen Actively: Pay full attention to the speaker, showing that you value their input.
2. Encourage Participation: Invite everyone to share their ideas and opinions in discussions.
3. Be Non-Judgmental: Respond to all contributions with respect, avoiding negative reactions.
4. Provide Constructive Feedback: Offer helpful and supportive feedback, focusing on solutions rather than criticism.
5. Model Openness: Share your own thoughts and vulnerabilities to set an example for others.

For Managers

As a manager, by creating an atmosphere where team members feel comfortable speaking up, you enable a flow of diverse ideas and solutions, leading to better decision-making and increased team cohesion. For example, in team meetings, make it a point to invite everyone to share their thoughts and ensure that all voices are heard. You might say, "I want to hear from everyone on this matter. Your input is valuable, and there are no wrong ideas." Addressing concerns without judgment encourages a culture of trust and continuous improvement.

For Individual Contributors

As an individual contributor, showing your peers that you value their contributions helps create an inclusive and dynamic work environment. Suppose a colleague is hesitant to share a new idea, fearing it might be dismissed. Encourage them by saying, "I think your idea has potential and could really help us. Let's discuss it further." This supportive approach not only boosts their confidence but also enriches your team's creative processes.

For Home Life

At home, encouraging an environment of open and honest communication is key. Imagine your child is afraid to discuss a poor grade with you. Instead of reacting negatively, you could say, "Thank you for sharing this with me. Let's talk about what happened and how we can work together to improve." This response shows empathy and support, helping your child feel understood and motivated to do better.

TAKE ACTION: This week, make a point of inviting in and valuing the input of your team members, peers, or family members.

RM13. Be Humble

Practicing humility is a powerful way to enhance your relationships and build a positive environment. This activity involves recognizing the contributions of others, maintaining a modest view of your own achievements, and giving credit where it is due.

How to Do It:
1. Share Credit: Highlight the contributions of others when discussing successes.
2. Express Gratitude: Regularly thank those who support and assist you.
3. Downplay Personal Achievements: Focus on the team or family effort rather than individual success.
4. Praise Publicly: Acknowledge others' contributions in meetings or family gatherings.
5. Encourage Others: Support and encourage the achievements and successes of those around you.

For Managers
As a manager, demonstrating humility can foster a culture of collaboration and respect. For instance, when celebrating a successful project, highlight the efforts of your team members rather than your leadership. You might say, "Our success on this project is thanks to everyone's hard work and dedication. Sarah's innovative ideas and John's attention to detail were particularly crucial." By attributing success to your team, you create an environment where everyone feels valued and motivated.

For Individual Contributors

As an individual contributor, recognizing your peers' contributions and downplaying your own shows that you value your team's success, not just your own. Suppose your team completes a challenging project ahead of schedule. Instead of focusing on your contributions, say, "This success is really a testament to everyone's hard work. Peep's creative solutions and Hugo's organizational skills made a huge difference."

For Home Life

At home, humility and praising your children or spouse for their achievements and efforts reinforces their value and importance, creating a supportive and encouraging family environment. For example, if you receive a promotion at work, you might say, "I couldn't have achieved this without your support and understanding. You all make it possible for me to do my best."

TAKE ACTION: This week, practice humility by sharing credit for success with a colleague, team member, or family member.

ABOUT THE AUTHORS

Kevin Kruse is globally recognized as an expert in leadership and culture, and is a *New York Times* bestselling author of several books including *Great Leaders Have No Rules, Employee Engagement 2.0,* and *15 Secrets Successful People Know About Time Management.* As the founder of several multimillion dollar technology companies, Kevin has won both Inc 500 awards for fast growth and Best Place to Work awards for great culture.

Evan Watkins is the author of *Team Emotional Intelligence 2.0: The Four Essential Skills of High Performing Teams,* and is a recognized expert in EQ and leadership. At LEADx, Evan leads the Leadership Development Community of Practice, an active group with over 1,000 members worldwide.

LEARN MORE

LEADx® is a leading provider of emotional intelligence assessments and training. Only LEADx offers free EQ assessments, flexible workshop options, and digital coaching to help you turn your knowledge into habits.

If you would like to bring EQ workshops to your organization, or would like to personally become a certified EQ trainer and coach, contact us at:

Web: www.LEADx.org/EQ

Email: info@leadx.org

Phone: (267) 702-6760

The LEADx Emotional Intelligence Habits™ Certification Program

Interested in delivering the Emotional Intelligence Habits™ workshop yourself? You can get certified through LEADx. LEADx will equip you with the materials, resources, and expertise you need to deliver a world-class EQ workshop.

> **Who It's For:** In-house trainers, facilitators, coaches, and independent consultants.

> **How It Works:** First, experience the full workshop as a participant. Then, learn how to facilitate the curriculum and roll out the program from a LEADx EQ-Certified Expert.

> **The Highest-Value Participant Kit Available:** Includes 3 months support from a LEADx EQ-certified coach, EQ Assessment, EQ book, 52 Strategies Job Aid, and the 3-month LEADx EQ e-Learning Module.

LEADx®

LEADx Certified EQ Facilitator

To learn more and see our pricing, scan the QR code

The LEADx Emotional Intelligence Habits™ Public Workshop

The Emotional Intelligence Habits™ Workshop is engaging, practical, and application-focused. Program participants:

> - learn the **business case** for EQ
> - take an **EQ assessment** to identify EQ strengths and growth areas
> - **practice the 4 core EQ skills** using 52 proven strategies
> - **create a personal action plan** to achieve their goals
> - **get access to an EQ expert coach for 12 weeks**

Clients love our program for its:

> - **6-hour virtual format (flexible)**
> - **Participant kit:** Includes EQ Assessment, EQ Book, 52 Strategies Job Aid, 3 months access to an EQ-certified coach and the LEADx EQ e-Learning Module
> - **"LEADx EQ" digital badge:** After completion of the workshop.

To reserve seats in our public workshop, scan the QR code ❯

LEADx®
Emotional Intelligence Habits

You can also work with one of our LEADx EQ Facilitators to deliver a program at your organization.

Contact us to learn more:

Email: support@leadx.org | **Phone:** (267) 702-6760

The LEADx Emotional Intelligence Habits® Keynote

Book the Author: Kevin Kruse is the Founder and CEO of LEADx, a New York Times bestselling author of ten books, and a Forbes leadership columnist with over 25 million views.

Kruse's EQ keynote explores how to develop high EQ habits that drive personal and professional success. This engaging, motivational presentation covers the foundational information around EQ, and inspires learners to dive deeper. Participants will:

> Learn what EQ is and why it matters

> Understand the four core skills of EQ (self-awareness, self-management, social awareness, relationship management)

> Receive a copy of *Emotional Intelligence: 52 Strategies* and take our EQ self-assessment

Ready to learn more about Kevin Kruse's Emotional Intelligence Habits® Keynote?

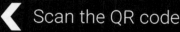 Scan the QR code